Dynamics of Contemporary
Border Management in Zimbabwe
Challenges, Benefits and Prospects

Adonis & Abbey Publishers Ltd

St James House
13 Kensington Square,
London, W8 5HD
United Kingdom

Website: http://www.adonis-abbey.com
E-mail Address: editor@adonis-abbey.com

Nigeria:
Suites C4 – C6 J-Plus Plaza
Asokoro, Abuja, Nigeria
Tel: +234 (0) 7058078841/08052035034

British Library Cataloguing-in-Publication Data
A catalogue record for this book is available from the British Library

ISBN: 978-1-906704-90-2

Dynamics of Contemporary Border Management in Zimbabwe
Challenges, Benefits and Prospects

Edited By

Solomon Muqayi & Charity Manyeruke

Notes on the contributors

1. **Dr Solomon Muqayi** is currently a Senior Lecturer in the Department of Political and Administrative Studies. He specialises in international relations, political science, border management and regional integration. He holds a PhD in International Relations (University of Zimbabwe), MSc in International Relations (University of Zimbabwe) and BSc in Public Administration (University of Zimbabwe). He has published widely in peer reviewed academic journals on Zimbabwe's foreign relations, political economy, political parties and democracy. Muqayi is an author of an article entitled; "The Impact of the Tokyo International Conference on African Development (TICAD) in Promoting Socio-economic Development in Zimbabwe." Journal of African Foreign Affairs. 5(3), 5-26.

2. **Professor Charity Manyeruke** is a Professor of Political Science and International Relations at the University of Zimbabwe. She holds a PhD in International Relations (University of Zimbabwe), MSc in International Relations (University of Zimbabwe) and BSc in Politics and Administration (University of Zimbabwe). She has published widely on International relations, African politics and political economy. Manyeruke is the author of a chapter on "Agricultural Subsidies: Hope for the Zimbabwean?' in Resilience Under Siege, the Zimbabwean Economy, Politics and Society edited by Chitando, E., Nyakudya, M. and Phiri, G. (Cambridge Scholars Publishing).

3. **Professor Innocent Chirisa** is currently the Deputy Dean in the Faculty of Social Studies at the University of Zimbabwe. He holds a PhD in Rural and Urban Planning (University of Zimbabwe), MSc in Rural and Urban Planning and BSc in Rural and Urban Planning (University of Zimbabwe).

4. **Dr Donald Chimanikire** is a senior International Relations lecturer at the University of Zimbabwe. He was the Political and Administrative studies Department chairperson. He has also held several other senior positions within the same institution; former Director of the Institute of Development Studies, former Chairperson of the Department of International Relations and Social Development Studies. He was, for a long time, a member of the Executive Committee of the Organization for Social Science Research in Eastern and Southern Africa (OSSREA), based in Addis Ababa, Ethiopia.

5. **Dr Lawrence Mhandara** is a Senior Lecturer at the University of Zimbabwe. He holds a PhD in Peace Studies (Durban University of Technology), MSc International Relations (University of Zimbabwe) and BSc Honours in Political Science (University of Zimbabwe).

6. **Dr Charles Mutasa** holds a PhD in International Relations (University of Zimbabwe), MSc Population Studies (University of Zimbabwe) and BSc Honours in Political Science (University of Zimbabwe).

7. **Dr Felistas, R. Zimano** is a Part-Time lecturer at Great Zimbabwe University. She holds a PhD in Management and Public Administration (University of KwaZulu Natal) and MSc International Relations (University of Zimbabwe) among other qualifications.

8. **Dr Alouis Chilunjika** is a Senior Lecturer at Midlands State University's Department of Politics and Public Management. He holds a in Public Administration (University of Johannesburg), Masters in Pu blic Administration (University of Zimbabwe and a BSc Honours Degree in Public Administration (University of Zimbabwe).

9. **Dr Rosemary Kasimba** is currently a Senior Lecturer in the Department of Sociology at the University of Zimbabwe. She holds a PhD in Sociology (Rhodes University), MSc in Sociology and Anthropology and BSc in Sociology (University of Zimbabwe).

10. **Sharon Hofisi** is a Lecturer at the University of Zimbabwe. He is also a lawyer. He is a PhD candidate with the University of Pretoria. He holds an MSc in International Relations (University of Zimbabwe), LLM (University of Zimbabwe) and LLB (University of Zimbabwe).

11. **Oripha Chimwara** is a Lecturer in the Department of Political and Administrative Studies at the University of Zimbabwe. She holds an MSc in International Relations (University of Zimbabwe) and BSc Honours in Political Science (University of Zimbabwe).

12. **Abraham Rajab Matamanda** holds degrees in BSc (Hons) Rural and Urban Planning and MSc Social Ecology, both from the University of Zimbabwe. His areas of research are urbanisation, sustainability, environmental planning, rural development, and the planning of cities and towns.

Table of Contents

CHAPTER ONE

Introduction:
An Overview of Border Management in Zimbabwe

Solomon Muqayi and Charity Manyeruke

Introduction

This book focuses on outlining the impact of border management programmes in addressing the challenges faced at the Zimbabwean borders. Zimbabwe is a landlocked country, centrally situated in the southern part of Africa and shares borders with South Africa (to the South), Mozambique (to the East), Zambia (to the North) and Botswana (to the West) (Government of Zimbabwe, 2016:7). Article 66(2b) of the Common Market for Eastern and Southern Africa (COMESA) Treaty states that "the Member States shall consult each other on the establishment of common border posts and take such steps as may be deemed appropriate to ensure that goods exported or imported through common frontiers pass through the competent and recognized Customs Offices and along approved routes". In line with the COMESA Treaty and other international laws, the Republic of Zimbabwe has therefore established 15 border posts and three big airports namely Robert Gabriel Mugabe International Airport, Victoria Falls Airport and Joshua Mqabuko Nkomo Airport (Shayanowako, 2013). The major border posts that connect Zimbabwe and her neighbouring countries include: borders with Zambia- Chirundu border post, Kanyemba border post, Kariba border post and Victoria Falls border post; borders with Mozambique- Forbes border post, Mount Silinda border post, Mukumbura border post, Nyamapanda border post and Sango border post; border with the Republic of South Africa- Beitbridge border post; and borders with Botswana- Kazungula border post, Pandamatenga border post, Plumtree border post, Maitengwe border post and Mphoengs border post (Government of Zimbabwe, 2017).

The busiest border post in Zimbabwe is the Beitbridge border post which is on the North-South Corridor and is a very important border crossing between Zimbabwe and South Africa. The average number of trucks crossing Beitbridge border post is 1136 trucks daily (Government of the Republic of South Africa, 2017). About 15 000 people transit Beitbridge border post daily, with the figures rising to 30 000 during peak periods (Muleya, 2018). Beitbridge border post connects many southern African countries such as Mozambique, Zimbabwe, South Africa, Zambia, Democratic Republic of Congo, Malawi, Lesotho and Swaziland, among others. The second busiest border post is the Chirundu One Stop Border Post (OSBP) which connects Zimbabwe and other Southern and Eastern countries such as Zambia, Democratic Republic of Congo (DRC), Malawi, Kenya, Burundi and Rwanda, among others (Government of Zimbabwe, 2017). Chirundu OSBP, Beitbridge and all other Zimbabwe's border posts play a critical role on the North-South corridor, a programme which was designed to expedite the movement of goods, people and services in Southern and Eastern Africa. Generally, borders determine industrial growth, national security and regional integration, among others. This can be supported by a SADC Report (2011:14) that states that state interests at the border include enforcement of immigration requirements, protection of national security, enforcement of export and import export restrictions and prohibitions, recording cross-border statistics, collection of revenue, and enforcement of sanitary and phytosanitary measures and technical standards. Zimbabwe's Industrial Development Policy (2012- 2016) highlights that lack of adequate control of incoming goods at border posts is allowing a lot of imports to be brought in without paying duties. This deprives the Government of the much needed revenue and also renders locally manufactured goods uncompetitive. Government will tighten the boarders and close the loopholes on smuggling .... governme nt will also review duties on a number of products and duty free allowance that individuals can bring into the country (Government of Zimbabwe, 2012:21). Given the importance of the key role played by borders, interestingly, little however has been studied and written about border management and the benefits and challenges faced at Zimbabwe's border posts. This is notwithstanding the fact that these border posts play a critical role towards Zimbabwe's politics and economy. This book therefore gives recommendations and strategies that are helpful towards the improvement of the management of borders as well as border policies in Zimbabwe.

Defining Borders, Border Management and Related Dynamics

A border is a place, generally between two countries, where goods and travellers are inspected ... land border checkpoints (land ports of entry) can be contrasted with the immigration and customs facilities at international airports, seaports, and other ports of entry (Merriam-Webster Dictionary, 2016). Article 1(2) of the Southern African Development Community (SADC) Protocol on the Facilitation of Movement of Persons defines a border as "Any common land border between any two Member States, or any airport used for flights within the Region, or sea port used for trans-shipment connections (SADC 1997:2). Borders are more than just barriers to free trade and are more important to economic (inter)activity than economics is apt or willing to tell us (Houtum, 1998:7). A border is an instrument used in the interest of economic policies, and yields the best results in terms of welfare, nationalisation and internationalisation (Houtum, 1998:7). A border is a central component to the concept of state sovereignty and statehood. Borders demarcate states and define a zone in which a state exercises territorial authority, integrity and jurisdiction that includes various processes such as development, enforcement and application of laws and policies (Ladley and Simmonds, 2007:6-11). Thus, a border can define a state in terms of geographical and legal terms. It is also noted in this book that borders are one of the most fundamental components of a state which require effective management and monitoring.

Border management is defined as the administration of borders that usually relates to the procedures regulating activities and the rules that guide cross-border activities (MacKay, 2008). Border management refers to coordinated approach by border control agencies, both international and domestic, in the context of seeking greater efficiencies over managing travel and trade flows while maintaining a balance with compliance requirements (Aniszewski, 2009:01). Border control means measures adopted by a country to regulate and monitor its borders ... It regulates the entry and exit of people, animals and goods across a country's border. It aims at fighting terrorism and detecting the movement of criminals across the borders (US Legal, 2018).

Border management is one of the crucial aspects shaping international political economy. Different aspects of border management are driven at various levels such as global, regional and national levels (MacKay, 2008). Zimbabwe's border management policies are highly influenced by policies and programmes set by the Southern African Development Community (SADC) and COMESA regional organisations, and these policies and programmes include Border Efficient Management System (BEMS), Integrated Border Management (IBM) and One Stop Border Post (OSBP). Accordingly, effective management of border programmes and policies has a direct influence on the flow of imports and exports.

Generally, all goods and services entering a country pass through the borders. Borders are therefore used as a strategic point to prohibit foreign goods and services (MacKay, 2008). A border is a place where compliance with national legislation in such areas as safety and security, commercial policy, customs procedures, agriculture quarantine, environment and immigration takes place (Aniszewski, 2009). Protectionism is mainly enforced at the borders so as to shelter domestic producers and local businesses from stiff international competition (Jones and Rosenblum, 2013). The most common types of protectionism that occur at the borders involve tariff and non-tariff barriers. The application of exorbitant import tariffs acts as a measure to discourage or prohibit external suppliers to supply their goods and services since high tariff rates adversely impact on profitability (Mubaiwa, 2013). Border protectionism is also enforced through the application of NTBs such as border delays, out-dated technology, multiple inspections and searches, administration bureaucracy and harassment (physical, psychological and mental) of traders. Border protectionism has several negative effects such as retaliation by neighbouring countries, long queues at the borders, congestion at the borders, scaring potential foreign investors, restricting local consumers to local products only and lack of competition in the domestic markets (Doyle et al 2011). This book therefore provides strategies, recommendations and solutions that could be implemented by the Zimbabwean government in order to address challenges faced at the borders.

Structure of the book

This book contains ten chapters that provide a broad spectrum and understanding of the dynamics of border management in Zimbabwe. These chapters were contributed by a variety of authors from various disciplines and institutions such as universities, think tanks, government offices and research institutions in Zimbabwe and abroad. The central focus of the various chapters compiled in this book is to evaluate the challenges, benefits and prospects for border management in Zimbabwe and the book chapters also give the recommendations and strategies that could be implemented to ensure sustainability in the management of Zimbabwe's borders. This book provides the link between border management and the following major themes: human trafficking, drug trafficking, border security, trade facilitation, globalization, political economy, customs clearance systems. Overall, proper implementation and execution of border management programmes and projects could help towards promote the reduction of revenue leakages, addressing the challenge of porous borders, reduction or elimination of unnecessary border delays, long queues, bureaucracy, reduction of drug trafficking and human trafficking, among others.

In chapter one, Solomon Muqayi and Charity Manyeruke give an overview of the book on contemporary border management. In chapter two, Solomon Muqayi gives an evaluation of the relevance of the Zimbabwean Border Efficiency Management System (BEMS) in achieving the international border management standards. BEMS is centred on improving efficiency in the management of border operations. In order to improve the management of borders, there is a need to improve the way of managing the operations at the borders. This chapter notes that BEMS is centred on the following key operational issues: operational structures; Information and Communication Technology (ICT); signage; help desk; rationalisation of border agencies; pre-clearance; One Stop Border Post (OSBP); and Integrated Border Management (IBM). This study, therefore, discusses these operational issues in detail. The study adopts qualitative research methods in the data gathering process. The chapter observes that there are weak customs clearance systems and facilities within the Zimbabwe customs at the country's main borders. For instance, technology, which could play a fundamental role in combating corruption as it increases transparency and accountability, especially through e-governance facilities, is not fully utilised. In order to improve the implementation of BEMS in Zimbabwe, a number of measures have to be undertaken and these include adopting appropriate legal and organizational frameworks, equipping personnel with contemporary training programmes, improving infrastructure and putting in place information and data exchange programmes.

In Chapter three, Felistas R. Zimano, Donald Chimanikire & Alouis Chilunjika give an outline of Border management Systems (BMS). An array of tried measures to alleviate transit challenges that build into BMS are documented in literature. Developing countries like Zimbabwe, which still face multiple border related challenges can draw lessons from such tried BMS. Countries face border related problems in unique ways due to varying underlying factors like historical background, economic levels, technological levels, country location, and government policies among other things. As such, this chapter presents seven amalgamated measures being utilised and envisioned by various countries. By bringing an array of options to the table, this chapter intends to stimulate scholars' and policymakers' mental power. Out of these, policymakers can brainstorm and come up with custom BMS applicable to border challenges experienced in their countries. This chapter also offers insights into border related challenges that are yet to be experienced in some developing countries. Such insights, if embraced, can help policymakers to put in order contemporary BMS to curtail such challenges even before they crop up in their countries. The style used herein is predominantly a review of relevant literature. Through the literature review, a case study on Zimbabwe's BMS is built and judicious BMS ideas from various parts of the world are brought to the fore.

In chapter four, Innocent Chirisa and Abraham Rajab Matamanda examine the spatial and physical planning considerations and implications of border management in Zimbabwe. This examination is significant for Zimbabwe because the understanding of dynamics around and along borderlands is a critical issue which has the potential to increase the collective power of those within them by providing the potential for organisation and preventing the diffusion of effort and energy. Qualitative research design informs the study where data has been collected from both primary and secondary sources. It emerges that borderlands in the country are associated with various challenges which are escalated by the geo-political and economic crisis which have been prevalent since the early 2000s. The study outlines the gross deficit of infrastructure and basic services which characterise border towns such as Chirundu, Beitbridge and Nyamapanda showing marginalisation of such spaces with regards to spatial and physical planning. Citizens are also vulnerable to wildlife which damages their crops as well as posing a threat on human life. Disparities in development is illustrated and explained among neighbouring countries and the implications on tourist benefits, for example, the Greater Limpopo Trans-frontier Conservation area where tourists are more on the South African side owing to a developed infrastructure on that side. The chapter concludes that spatial and physical considerations and border management in Zimbabwe is an area that requires committed effort and attention from the government if sustainability is to be achieved as espoused in the different conventions and protocols which guide and regulate sustained socio-economic development of various sectors in the country.

In chapter five, Solomon Muqayi sought to assess the relevance of the Automated System for Customs Data (ASYCUDA) in promoting trade facilitation. ASYCUDA was adopted by the Zimbabwe Revenue Authority (ZIMRA), Customs Division, at Zimbabwe border posts, with specific reference to the improvement of the following issues: border management, custom clearance systems and reduction of revenue leakages. Literature review was carried out on the topic under study which revealed the strides that ASYCUDA has made in curbing customs administrative challenges. There was however a gap in the literature on the limitations of ASYCUDA as an automated system. A qualitative research was undertaken and a case study of the Zimbabwe Revenue Authority was used. Primary data was obtained using interviews and secondary data in the form of reports, customs journals, periodicals and publications was used. A total of seventeen respondents were interviewed from different organizations related to the topic understudy, ten being managers whilst the other seven comprised of clearing agents. The respondents were selected using purposive sampling. The respondents from ZIMRA were selected based on their work experience, expertise and knowledge in the area under study whilst clearing agents were selected based on the size of their companies with regard to their clientele base. Data was analyzed through data reduction, coding, categorization and identification of common themes. The study revealed that ZIMRA faced challenges and that ASYCUDA has been effective in curbing these challenges. It was therefore concluded that ASYCUDA has been effective in curbing customs administrative challenges in ZIMRA. The study also identified challenges that impede the effectiveness of ASYCUDA in curbing customs administrative challenges. Recommendations were therefore made in line with these findings as to how these challenges can be addressed in order to effectively utilize ASYCUDA.

In Chapter six, Charity Manyeruke indicates that security is a very sensitive aspect which covers a lot of subjects including human security and even cargo. The magnitude of its importance calls for a lot of attention needed at the border to ensure the safety of human beings and their goods. Beitbridge border post is one of the busiest border posts in Southern of Africa and due to economic challenges that Zimbabwe has been facing a number of people have been involved in some form of cross border trading. Beitbridge Bporder Post handles the largest volume of traffic in Southern Africa yet there has been no significant infrastructure development in the past couple of years. Incidences of smuggling and other illegal activities have increased and this has compromised security and the general border management. The theory of territorial indivisibility highlights that states emphasise on security in their fight for sovereignty. On the other hand the theory on state building and border security argues that states through security seek to expand their influence over there territory. Surveillance of all port entries is one of the recommendations to this study.

Sharon Hofisi, in Chapter seven notes that Zimbabwe is a source, transit zone and destination for dangerous drugs is incontrovertible. Drivers dump their trucks carrying dagga at border posts. Zimbabweans frequently consume illicit brews such as Nipa/Kachasu, as well as dangerous medicinal drugs such as broncleer (Chipunza and Razemba 2017). There are some drugs from other countries such as zed which is believed, can destroy the consumer's teeth if the liquid gets to them. But the consumers seem like they do not even worry about the damage that can be done to their internal system. The important issue Hofisi considers is how Zimbabwe can use a multi-sector approach, including effective border control to alleviate the drug problem in a principled and comprehensive way. Such an approach should encourage government and civil society organizations to partner in mobilizing social resistance to drugs, protecting investigative journalists to speak out on politics-drugs issues and to ensure that CSOs, government institutions and academic institutions collaborate in drug-related researches. This means that states should entrench border control models that also involve different stakeholders who can assist in the training and capacitation of citizens and border control teams. This will enable the country to find best ways to align its laws with the constitution, reduce instances of drug trafficking and design effective border control measures.

In chapter 8, Charles Mutasa indicates that drug abuse and drug trafficking has been around for centuries, but with improved technology, drug smugglers have also become sophisticated and complicated in their evasion of porous border controls. For a less-developed country like Zimbabwe, which is still battling with poverty and economic stagnation, marginalized women and youths are used by the powerful drug barons and cartels as agents in the illicit drug trafficking business both within the country and across borders. In most schools and colleges, drug abuse has become a way of self-pacification in a land full of many socio-economic challenges, though unhealthy and destructive to many youths. This chapter looks at how drug trafficking and drug abuse is tearing down individual lives, groups, institutions and the country that could have seen better development than what is currently being experienced. Zimbabwe's economic doldrums, which are characterized by high rates of unemployment, migration and lack of social protection have not escaped the temptation of having an increasing number of youths and women joining the drug trafficking business in the region and internationally. A number of problems have been encountered as a result of the increase in cases of drug abuse within an environment that has no resources to respond to the plight. Some of the challenges of drug trafficking include increases in cases of mental health, loss of human lives, and family breakdowns, exacerbated by a civil society network and government departments that are failing to cope. The chapter thus recommends the need for a more coordinated approach, led by a Commission established to look into the illicit drug related issues in a transparent manner and reporting to parliament. There is need for better legislation, policies and strategies that emanates from the collective views of multi-stakeholders in government, the private sector and civil society. The urgent need to safeguard our porous borders from the smuggling of drugs into the country and the trafficking of the same drugs to other countries is well covered in the chapter.

Solomon Muqayi, in Chapter nine give an evaluation of the Integrated Border Management (IBM) programme in promoting contemporary border management at Zimbabwe's border posts. For Customs, IBM is about describing how improved regulatory efficiency and effectiveness can be realised through greater coordination between border agencies during policy development and operational activities, both domestically and internationally. This chapter considers the meaning of the IBM concept for the customs community in particular and border agencies in general. It provides an overview of the evolution of the concept, through explicating the globalization concept and how it has affected traditional definitions of borders, which serves as a theoretical underpinning for further policy development. As the IBM concept is broad and offers numerous interpretations, operational arrangements, such as joint mobile teams, hot pursuit, joint risk management, and targeting centres are not addressed, however the chapter analyses information exchange systems, in particular the Single Window that forms an intrinsic part of IBM. The chapter further focuses on institutional and some practical integrated border management frameworks developed in several countries, particularly Zimbabwe as part of an IBM implementation strategy as a measure to enhancing trade facilitation at Zimbabwe's borders.

In Chapter ten, Oripha Chimwara and Lawrence Mhandara give an outline of the relationship between border management and human smuggling in chapter six. Migration is embedded in the history of human society. There are convincing arguments that people have always moved from one place to the other in search of better lives. The process continued with the emergence of the state system and territorial boundaries. The process of globalisation has resulted in an unprecedented trend of migration from the less developed to the relatively developed countries. The challenge has however been the increase of illegal migration as legal migration fails to cope with the ever-escalating demand for migration. One contributing source of irregular migration is human smuggling. Although human smuggling is not novel, it is a menace to the extent that international law is categorically clear on its criminal and illegal status. Departing from the premise that human smuggling is under-researched in Southern Africa, this chapter examines the elements of human smuggling from Zimbabwe to South Africa through Beitbridge border post. Using a qualitative methodological orientation that relied on key informant interviews and informal conversations, the research finds that migration increased because of the economic and political forces in Zimbabwe that constrained individual choices and contributed to insidious forms of everyday suffering. This prompted a high demand for migration to relatively stable countries, to which South Africa became the preferred destination. Unfortunately, the immigration policies of South Africa fell short of satisfying the ever-increasing demand for migration among Zimbabweans leading to illegal entry through smuggling. Cross-border transporters, fellow immigrants, families and friends working with corrupt border management officials at either side of the border post are key actors in the smuggling process. Holism is required in countering smuggling because of its potential to expose smuggled migrants to the impunity of traffickers in South Africa. In addition, the official securitisation discourse around Zimbabwean migrants is a potent risk factor that can contaminate the bilateral relations between the two neighbouring states.

References

Government of Zimbabwe, 2017. Official Ports of Entry for Zimbabwe. https://pflanzengesundheit.julius-kuehn.de/dokumente/upload/1eb7f_zw3-einlassstellen.pdf

Government of the Republic of South Africa, 2017. Border Posts/Ports of Entry. http://www.safiri.co.za/lpfdb/cross-border-border posts.html

Muleya, T. 2018. 106 000 Travellers Pass Through Beitbridge. The Herald. https://www.herald.co.zw/106-000-travellers-pass-through-beitbridge/

Government of Zimbabwe, 2018. National Budget Statement for 2018. Government of Zimbabwe: Harare.

SADC, 2011. Draft Guidelines on the Coordinated Border Management. SADC: Gaborone.

Treaty Establishing the African Economic Community. 2014. Accessed 5
June 2015, from http://www.au.int/en/sites/default/files/TREATY
_ESTABLISHING_THE_AFRICAN_ECONOMIC_COMMUNIT
Y.pdf

Ministry of Industry and Commerce, 2012. Industrial Development
Policy (2012-2016). Government of Zimbabwe: Harare

Government of Zimbabwe, 2012. National Trade Policy (2012-2016).
Ministry of Industry and Commerce: Harare.

Government of Zimbabwe, 2016. Zimbabwe Foreign Trade and
Investment Guidelines 2016. Reserve Bank of Zimbabwe: Harare.

SADC, 1997. Protocol on the Facilitation of Movement of Persons.
SADC: Gaborone.

Houtum, H.E. 1998. The Development of Cross-Border Economic
Relations: A theoretical and empirical study of the influence of the
state border on the development of cross-border economic relations
between firms in border regions of the Netherlands and Belgium.
ThelaThesis Publishers: Amsterdam

Macmillan Dictionary, 2017. https://www.macmillandictionary.com/dic
tionary/british/border-crossing.

Merriam Webster Dictionary, 2016. https://www.merriam webster.com/
dictionary/border.

Aniszewski, S. 2009. "Coordinated Border Management". WCO Researc
h Paper, 2(1), 1-18.

US Legal, 2018. Border Management. https://definitions.uslegal.com/b/
border-control/

Jones, C.V. and Rosenblum, R.M 2013. US Customs and Border
Protection: Trade Facilitation, Enforcement and Security. Washingto
n: Congressional Research Paper.

Mubaiwa, S. 2013. An Evaluation of Trade Facilitation Measures
Implemented by the Common Market for Eastern and Southern
Africa (COMESA): The Case of Chirundu One Stop Border Post.
Bindura: Bindura University of Science and Education.

Ladley, A and Simmonds, N. 2007. The Border and Customs in the 21st
Century: Or How to Outfox the Future. Wellington: University of
Wellington.

MacKay, A. 2008. Border Management and Gender: Gender and Security
Sector Reforms Toolkit. Geneva: DCAF.

CHAPTER TWO

The Relevance of the Zimbabwean Border Efficiency Management System (BEMS) in Achieving International Border Management Standards

Solomon Muqayi

Introduction

Border management is often defined as the administration of borders by a 'professionally trained security apparatus with responsibilities, powers, functional mandates and a professional identity separate and distinct from other security providing structures' (Marenin 2006:17). The rules, techniques and procedures within any border security system vary depending on the national and regional context, the organisational dynamics, and the multiple 'rationalities' under consideration (Hills 2006a, 2006b). In war-torn societies, poorly governed and weak states, border management responds to a peace building and developmental rationality. Borders perform a crime-fighting and a trade function but are also part of building the international personality and territorial integrity of societies. Increasingly, border management also serves an internal security rationality whereby the international community uses border management as a strategy to protect populations from the consequences of the 'regressive developmental malaise' (Carnegie Commission cited in Duffield, 2003:307). That is, non-conventional and transnational forms of crime (including illegal flows of people, goods, capital and services) that flourish on the basis of local and regional socio-economic, political and environmental insecurities, and the privatisation of conflict. The 'War on Terror' has added impetus to the use of border management as a foreign tool to obtain domestic security due to the increasing association that can be found in many policy circles between terrorist networks and organised crime activities (Ioannides and Celador, 2011: 416-419). As a result of the changing trends in border management regionally and internationally, Zimbabwe has embraced multifarious border efficiency management strategies such as IBM, ASYCUDA systems and police and intelligence inspections, smart cameras and scanners amongst others in order to ensure efficiency in managing border posts for the purposes of facilitating trade, swift movement of goods, people and exchange of information through internet links among border posts.

Theoretical framework

Cross Border Theory

The cross border theory is a practice-oriented theoretical framework that is specifically developed for cross-border regional cooperation at policy-oriented level (Huxham and Vangen, 2006:67). Establishing, managing and designing this kind of cooperation is a complex and often unpredictable process that requires a well-thought out strategic approach. The cross border theory is a theory of action that offers useful support for pioneers in every phase of these processes. The cross border theory is not a conventional theory connecting cause and consequence, nor does it possesses predictive qualities (Van der Molen, 2011:79). But what does it offer? In bigger projects it is not surprising to use decision support systems when tackling contextual issues. Why are things proceeding the way they do? What is the correct strategy to use when the process needs to be adjusted? What tools do we have available for this task? These are the questions that need an additional theory of action. Up until now, this was not available. The cross border theory fills this omission.

The theory is not an 'instruction book', in the sense of: 'If this is the case, then do that' (Bardach (2001:67). It is a flexible theory of action for various relevant aspects of the border cooperative process offering pioneers meaningful points of attention and options for each stage of border cooperation. Accordingly the theory acts as an activity supporting system for complex and lengthy processes. The cross border theory is built around nine areas of attention among which the pioneer must divide his attention in smaller or greater amounts, during the development of the cooperative partnerships. According to Van der Molen (2011:80) these nine areas of attention are:

1. Determining position according to the stages described by;
2. Exploring and monitoring the context during the process;
3. Initiating and managing cooperative processes;

4. Establishing cooperative partnerships;
5. Further developing cooperative partnerships;
6. Addressing possible issues for joint policies;
7. Handling possible impact of administrators;
8. Handling the effects of state borders; and
9. Determining the appropriate legal form.

The cross border theory clearly defines the multiple level border cooperation between and among states regionally and internationally. Border cooperation, thus, includes bilateral exchanges of goods and services between states. However is not limited to trade cooperation but also movement of people from one country to another as well as other forms of significant cooperation. The concept of cooperation has been subject of many publications in the past decades. For a definition of the term cooperation we refer to (Bardach, 2001). He defines cooperation as "any joint activity of two or more organizations, aimed at generating public value by working together instead of separately of each other." This definition is broad enough to cover a comprehensive range of governmental and non-governmental organizations and specific enough to exclude other types of activities between organizations. This study therefore works on the assumption of this definition as premised by the cross border theory. The poor economic situation prevailing in Zimbabwe has led to multiple and complex migration issues characterized by high levels of brain drain, cross border mobility, and irregular migration. Breadwinners and in many cases entire families have migrated to other centres or across borders in search of better employment opportunities. Skill areas affected include, but are not limited to medicine, education, engineering, surveying, architecture, audiology, veterinary medicine and forensic science. The loss of skills is of growing concern as it has negatively impacted on service delivery. While the foregoing illustrates the magnitude of the migration challenges that Zimbabwe has been facing, the capacity of the Government of Zimbabwe (GoZ) to manage these multi-faceted migration issues so as to reduce the negative aspects of migration and enhance its positive impact are usually constrained by lack of a comprehensive and coherent legal, institutional and policy framework for implementing migration practices in an integrated manner. Up until March 2008 there was no institutional framework that spearheaded the day to day migration and development issues within the GoZ. Migration issues were dealt with by officials in several stakeholder ministries, with no or limited coordination and without following a common strategy. The core responsibilities of these officials were not related to migration and development. Consequently, migration and development tasks tended to lag behind in terms of priority. The lack of adequate data and analysis of the nature and extent of factors driving migration further limited the ability of the government to devise appropriate policies and programmes focusing on the management of migration for national benefit.

Research Methodology

The researcher employed the qualitative approach for data collection and analysis. According to Borg and Gall (1989:385), a qualitative approach focuses on meaning, experiences and social realities which are purposively selected and observed by the researcher. Based on a theoretical or judgemental approach, the study depended upon a number of data sources that included documents, research studies, articles, electronic and print media, books on border management and legislative documents. Key informant interviews were also incorporated as data collection method. Strategic and key interviews were conducted with strategic people with relevant information on border management. Thus were drawn from the Zimbabwe Revenue Authority (ZIMRA), Ministry of Foreign Affairs and International Trade, Ministry of Industry and Commerce, Zim-Trade, Common Market for Eastern and Southern Africa (COMESA) Secretariat as well as Shipping and Forwarding Association of Zimbabwe (SIFAZ). The researcher also reviewed articles and primary reports from ZIMRA, Ministry of Foreign Affairs and International Trade, Ministry of Industry and Commerce, Zim-Trade, Common Market for Eastern and Southern Africa (COMESA) Secretariat as well as Shipping and Forwarding Association of Zimbabwe (SIFAZ). Data on the cases studied was collected through an electronic search on the application of Border Efficiency Management Strategies which were implemented by the GoZ.

The researcher enhanced validity and reliability by citing articles and other sources that are authentic and credible. Secondary sources of data were as well complimented by information that was ferreted from interviews with well-informed key informants from ZIMRA and other line institutions or stakeholders in border management in Zimbabwe. The researcher applied content analysis for analysing data collected from interviews, documents and observations. Collected data was carefully categorised into themes which were coded and analysed for internal logic and coherence. This approach was deployed in the fine-grained analysis of the existing documentation on BEMS and border management strategies to be able to draw meaningful conclusions on the strategies used by the Zimbabwean government to effectively and proficiently manage borders.

Discussion of Findings

Historical Development of BEMS in Zimbabwe

BEMS is a programme that was initiated by the COMESA regional bloc. The implementation of BEMS shows Zimbabwe's compliance with international border management standards. The Zimbabwe border management agenda includes the following aspects: coordinated border management framework, One Stop Border Post, Single Window, customs and customs cooperation arrangements, customs to business cooperation arrangements and customs to other border agencies cooperation arrangements (ZIMRA, 2012). BEMS is a broad programme with various sub-components. One of the key informant interviewees in explaining the BEMS noted that "BEMS is the mother programme whereas the child programmes are: OSBP, IBM, and ASYCUDA, among others." The implementation of BEMS at Zimbabwe's ports of entry has led to the establishment of the Chirundu OSBP and there were plans to establish more OSBPs.

BEMS is centred on improving efficiency in the management of border operations. In order to improve the management of borders, there is a need to improve the way of managing the operations at the borders. This study noted that BEMS is centred on the following key operational issues: (1) operational structures; (2) Information and Communication Technology (ICT); (3) signage; (3) help desk; (4) rationalisation of border agencies; (5) pre-clearance; (6) One Stop Border

Post (OSBP); and (7) Integrated Border Management (IBM). This Study, therefore, discusses these operational issues in detail.

Operational structures

Operational structures have to do with the physical infrastructural structures planted at the ports of entry (border posts and air ports). The major question here is: Do the structures allow faster movement of goods and people at the ports of entry? There is also a need to assess structures in order to find out whether they are user-friendly to traders, travellers and even the border clearance agencies themselves. Any person using the ports of entry should easily understand the setup of port of entry structures. This study noted that ports of entry and infrastructural structures should link. Thus, offices, roads and desks should be structured in a way that does not confuse travellers and traders. Desks at the ports of entry should be arranged in an orderly manner, for example, the immigration desk at should be at the first point and then followed by other departments such as ZIMRA and Port Health. Traders should first of all be given the right to cross the border before clearing their consignments. During the period covered by the study, it was observed that some of the ZIMRA offices at the Beitbridge offices were not linked especially when it comes to issues related to the importation of cars. The offices for clearing are quite divorced. Some offices were placed at the border whereas some offices were located at a place called Manica which is far away from the border. Thus, some processes such as car clearance by ZIMRA, CVR and CID were conducted at Manica while other processes such as the payments of import duties and other taxes were done at the border. Generally, there is a long distance between these offices. Thus, car traders were forced to hire taxis in order to get to the border so that they can make the highlighted payments. The office setup at Chirundu did not promote short turnaround times. This situation was the cause of huge financial costs to the car traders. Furthermore, the study also found that some bogus transport operators were robbing these car dealers since they were carrying money to make import duty payments at the border. The study noted that to generate revenue and minimise crime incidences, ZIMRA should, therefore, address these inconveniences by adhering to the requirements of BEMS programmes.

The Zimbabwe BEMS programme also focuses on port of entry operational structures such as the implementation or installation of non-intrusive systems (scanners) at selected ports. The programme also involves the construction of a traffic separation and channelling at the entry points. This study noted that non-intrusive systems (scanners) had been installed and made functional at the following ports of entry: (1) at the Robert Gabriel Mugabe International Airport (cargo terminal) there was an installation of palletised scanners; (2) at the Beitbridge border posts, the following types of scanners were installed: baggage scanner, mobile container scanner and re-locatable container scanner; (3) Plumtree border post: baggage scanners and mobile container scanners were installed; (4) Chirundu OSBP: mobile container scanners were installed. This study also noted that the Zimbabwean government was in the process of proceeding with the programme in order to install the following intrusive systems at the specified areas: (1) the installation of container depot scanners at Forbes and Nyamapanda; (2) the installation of radiation portals at the airports and border posts; (3) introduction of the Police Canine Unit with dogs at all ports of entry having been acquired for the scanning purposes. The installation of these modern day scanners helps to reduce the time spent during scanning of consignment thereby leading to reduced turnaround times. In addition to this, during the period covered by the study, there was a programme of fixing traffic separation- channelling at the border posts. At the Chirundu OSBP, demarcation of traffic in the following channels and lanes was being done: commercial traffic (trucks), buses and light commercial vehicles, private motor vehicles, pedestrian traffic and red and green route. Generally, the programme was adopted with the aim of decongesting the borders through improving quick and easy movement of traffic and people at the port of entry. This also helped to address the problem of border delays. This study, therefore, noted that Zimbabwe was fully supporting the implementation of BEMS programmes since the government was aligning the port of entry operational structures in line with the requirements of COMESA regional integration organisation. Thus, the GoZ should implement programmes that reduce border protectionism and at the same time enhance trade facilitation.

Entry Point Signage

This involves the establishment of signs at the ports of entry. Installation of signage at the ports of entry helps both transporters and pedestrians with fundamental information such as directions and procedures. During the period covered by the study, there was an Inter-ministerial Committee (committee composed of stakeholders from various Ministries and governmental departments) which was established in order to implement the BEMS programme. The Inter-ministerial Committee proposed to install the most appropriate and modern signage systems at the ports of entry. The signages were chosen in relation to the Modular Curved Framed Technology (MCFT) signage system (ZIMRA, 2013). Three classes of signage that were to be installed at the Zimbabwe ports of entry are: directional signage, procedural signage and informative signage (ZIMRA 2013). During the period under study, notable progress was made by ZIMRA and its related authorities were advertising for tenders in order to hire the companies that were to fix the signage at various ports of entry, which is at border posts and air ports. This Study noted that there are several benefits associated with the establishment of port of entry signage and these are: (1) signage helps to reduce confusion for those crossing the border posts as well as those using the airports; (2) it reduces pressure on border clearance agencies in the sense that traders and travellers will not ask unnecessary questions, instead they will simply follow the information provided by the border signs; and (3) signage actually helps to reduce congestion at the ports of entry in the sense that transporters will not stop where they are not supposed to stop and they will also drive without asking for directions unnecessarily. This also leads to the reduction of time spent at the ports of entry. This study therefore noted that all of these stages help in addressing border barriers which hinder the development of a country's role in promoting free trade.

Information and Communication Technology (ICT)

This involves the establishment of technological infrastructure in order to facilitate the transfer of information and data. ICT involves the establishment of services such as internet, telephone land lines and cell phone networks at the ports of entry. Connectivity at the borders should be established in a way that ensures that offices and agencies are connected together. For instance, at Zimbabwe borders they use

ASYCUDA. The BEMS programme, therefore, ensures that government departments working at the borders are connected to ASYCUDA. During the period under study, it was noted that not all government departments working at the borders were connected to ASYCUDA. It was wholly accessed by ZIMRA but other departments such as Immigration, the ZRP and VID were not accessing ASYCUDA. Furthermore, at the Chirundu OSBP, it was also noted that Zimbabwean and Zambian computers were not networked together and this was slowing down the customs clearance system. It was also difficult to combat the incidents of fake documentation by bogus traders.

Zimbabwe adopted the Single Window concept at the borders as a mechanism to integrate workflow processes, procedures and business unit IT systems (ZIMRA 2013). During the period covered by the study, there were plans to implement the Single Window in two phases which are workflow processes Single Window and information lodgement Single Window. The proper implementation of Single Window helps to improve the customs clearance processes. This study noted that the government should address the following in order to improve the border post ICT processes: (1) have a network database that would be accessed by governmental departments involved in the management of border operations; (2) the establishment of communication channels connecting revenue offices and head offices; (3) developing a system that is efficient in collecting, processing and distributing information in particular for activities and transactions that occur at the borders; (4) establishing consistent internet connections; and (5) designing a uniform automated information exchange on all border posts and airports. This study found that ASYCUDA is not uniformly installed at all Zimbabwean borders

Rationalisation of Border Agencies

During the period covered by this study, there was a considerable number of agencies at Zimbabwe's ports of entry. There was also an influx of bogus agencies at the border posts and this was causing confusion to travellers. The rationalisation of border agencies calls for the removal of unnecessary organisations, companies and agencies at the borders. The main emphasis of this rationalisation agenda is: Which agent should continue operating at the border and which should be removed in order to maintain rationality? Rationalisation, therefore, allows the elimination of duplication of efforts (Shayanowako, 2013). One of the major border activities that reflected duplication of effort was that of border inspections. There were various border agencies involved in inspections: ZIMRA, ZRP, the defence forces, CIO, Immigration and Veterinary Services. These departments were carrying out inspections individually thereby inspecting the same person or consignment for several instances. These haphazard inspections were embarrassing and often resulted in the harassment of traders and travellers. The GoZ should, therefore, appoint only a few departments to be involved in border inspections so as to promote rationality as well as avoiding duplication of effort.

Preclearance

This is a process whereby imports and exports are cleared before reaching the borders. When the actual consignment arrives at the borders, agencies will, therefore, be involved in minor activities such as conducting inspections, scanning and routine verification processes in order to find out the compatibility between the declared goods and the actual consignment. ZIMRA facilitates preclearance processes through the Automated System for Customs Data (ASYCUDA World). ASYCUDA World allows importers and importers to launch their consignment on the ZIMRA website before getting to the borders. ZIMRA can, therefore, conduct some valuation activities in advance thereby allowing the trader to make payments for his/her import duty charges. Indications from this are that preclearance helps to address border protectionist challenges such as border congestion and long queues. It also helps to reduce the time spent by traders at the ports of entry since the majority of activities are conducted online. However, this study noted that pre-clearance procedures pose negative effects on the jobs of border officials. It was noted that the introduction of preclearance exercises has caused ZIMRA to reduce the number of its border officers since there was a reduction of work to be carried out at the borders.

Challenges of BEMS

The major challenges affecting Zimbabwe's BEMS programme that were noted during the period covered by this study include: (1) the Zimbabwean government was taking long to establish the help desk at airport and border posts. The absence of the help desk was causing travellers and traders to be preyed upon by bogus agencies that were pretending to be helpers; (2) there were some building structures which were not compatible with the requirements of BEMS. For example the buildings at Forbes border post were so small that they could not allow the establishment of an OSBP. There was a need to put new structures and this was rather costly to the government; (3) some of the stakeholders taking part in the activities at the borders are resisting the implementation of BEMS necessarily because they are afraid of being evicted from the borders. For instance, the border agencies that are not contributing much relevance to border management, for example, multiple security agencies from various Ministries and government departments; (4) infrastructural challenges- the infrastructure on Zimbabwe's borders was not designed to cater for large volumes of trucks. The constantly increasing volumes of regional trade had led to the evolvement of multiple challenges at the border posts. For example, there was an entire need to construct separate roads at the Chirundu OSBP in order to accommodate big commercial trucks. In addition to that, the air conditioning machines at the Chirundu OSBP were completely damaged thereby exposing the border agencies to very hot atmospheric conditions; (5) financial challenges: Zimbabwe's BEMS programme was heavily constrained by financial shortages. Finance was required to establish infrastructural structures and attending COMESA meetings. The Zimbabwean government is not consistently attending to COMESA meetings. Furthermore, it has been sending a very small delegation to hold negotiations at COMESA thereby negatively affecting the intensity of the negotiations. This was bringing several challenges to Zimbabwe in the sense that its views and grievances were not properly presented; (6) the lack of adequate signage; and (7) the proliferation of bogus agencies. This was causing unnecessary bottlenecks and congestion at the airports and border posts.

Conclusion

Evaluating the implementation of the Zimbabwe's BEMS necessarily requires touching on a number of issues that go beyond the coordination challenge and that can be grouped under two sub-headings: SADC-related explanations and contextual conditions. Therefore, this study observed that offices, roads and desks should be structured in a way that does not confuse travellers and traders. Desks at the ports of entry should be arranged in an orderly manner, for example, immigration desk at the first point followed by other departments such as ZIMRA and Port Health.

This study observed that scanning systems had been installed and made functional at the following ports of entry at the Harare International Airport (cargo terminal) there was an installation of palletised scanners; at the Beitbridge border posts, the following types of scanners were installed: baggage scanner, mobile container scanner and re-locatable container scanner; Plumtree border post: baggage scanners and mobile container scanners were installed; Chirundu OSBP: mobile container scanners were installed. This study also noted that the Zimbabwean government was in the process of proceeding with the programme in order to install the following intrusive systems at the specified areas: The installation of container depot scanners at Forbes and Nyamapanda; the installation of radiation portals at the airports and border posts; introduction of the Canine Unit with dogs at all ports of entry having been acquired for the scanning purposes. The installation of these modern day scanners helps to reduce the time spent during scanning of consignment thereby leading to reduced turnaround times. In addition to this, during the period covered by the study, there was a programme of fixing traffic separation- channelling at the border posts. At the Chirundu OSBP, demarcation of traffic in the following channels and lanes was being done: commercial traffic (trucks), buses and light commercial vehicles, private motor vehicles, pedestrian traffic and Red and Green route. Generally, the programme was adopted with the aim of decongesting the borders through improving quick and easy movement of traffic and people at the port of entry. This also helped to address the problem of border delays. This Study, therefore, noted that Zimbabwe was fully supporting the implementation of BEMS programmes since the government was aligning the port of entry operational structures in line with the requirements of COMESA regional integration organisation.

Thus, the Zimbabwe government is relevant in implementing programmes that help in reducing border protectionism and at the same time enhancing trade facilitation.

The main factor to consider when analysing the effectiveness of efforts to develop functional border agencies in the region is the agenda guiding the SADC, which can be at odds with the needs on the ground. This situation is clearly illustrated by the SADC's visa regime vis-à-vis Zimbabwe, driven to a large extent by political and security imperatives resulting from the socioeconomic, developmental, trade concerns. Beginning in 2008, the visa liberalisation dialogue between the SADC states and the whole of Africa has been based on meeting 'stringent, non-negotiable conditions' in four 'blocks', of which only one went beyond security matters: (1) document security; (2) border control/management, migration and asylum (including re-admission agreements for the repatriation of illegal immigrants to countries of origin); (3) public order and security (including the fight against organised crime, corruption and terrorism), and (4) external relations and fundamental rights. As explained by the SADC report on Border Management in Southern Africa, the first three security-driven 'blocks' were more important for SADC countries when assessing region's progress in the visa liberalisation process.

Recommendations

The Zimbabwean government and its neighbouring COMESA/SADC member states are recommended to implement the following recommendations in order to improve the BEMS programme:

- Appointing a department or institution responsible for overall management of borders in Zimbabwe.
- Controlling and regulating cross-border activities as a way of ensuring peace and stability, and enhancing regional and continental integration
- Creating and maintaining automated data bases and information systems (both national, regional and international) on cross-border crimes, illegal movements and crime syndicates.

- Creating bilateral institutional framework that allows joint border management.
- Developing and adopting border management legislations and aligning them to regional standards.
- Developing radio networks to improve communication between border management/security personnel.
- Enabling joint border patrols to operate throughout the borders.
- Improving surveillance as well as acquiring equipment to detect smuggling activities carried out via bushes and rivers.
- Involving local communities in securing and maintaining borders.
- Militarizing or actively patrolling border crime hotspots.
- Providing border security personnel with radios, cell phones, patrol means, and fast communication and network channels to be used by border patrol officers.
- Setting up border criminal investigation units and training border security personnel in criminal investigation techniques.
- Standardizing, realigning and harmonizing border management techniques to meet regional border standards/guidelines.
- Understanding border characteristics and how they impact on management.
- Undertaking an assessment/analysis of border security threat focusing on matters such as trafficking trends, patterns, tactics, routes and traffickers' methods. This exercise should also assess the needs for equipment and skills.
- Adapting a strategic plan on border security and management that aims at, among other things, enhancing inter and intra-departmental agencies cooperation.

Reference

Aksoy, A.M., and Beghin, J.C. 2005. Global Agricultural Trade and Developing Countries. Washington: The World Bank.

Angwenyi, V. 2014. Competition Law and Regional Integration: The Common Market for Eastern and Southern Africa (COMESA). Munich: Ludwig-Maximilians University.

de Andrés, A. P. 2008. "West Africa under attack: drugs, organized crime and terrorism as the new threats to global security," UNISCI Discussion Papers, No. 16.

Hernández, D. J. 2007. "North America: Managing our Borders and the Perimeter," presentation made at the American University, Washington, D.C.

Ndayisenya, F. 2004. "Economic Impacts of Regulatory Convergence Between Canada and the United States," In Horizons,7:1 (June 2004), Canadian Policy Research Initiative.

Chibwesha, F. 2010. The Challenges of a Customs union: The Case of COMESA. Lusaka: University of Zambia.

Chipeta, C. 1998. Trade and Investment in Southern Africa: Towards Regional Economic Cooperation and Integration. Harare: SAPES Trust.

Chirisa, I. 2013. Housing and Stewardship in Peri-Urban Settlement in Zimbabwe: A Case Study of Ruwa and Epworth. Harare: University of Zimbabwe.

Churchill, G.A. 2009. Marketing Research: Methodological Foundations. London: Dryden Press.

Colman, D. 2001. The Common Agricultural Policy: In the Economics of the European Union. New York: Oxford University Press.

COMESA, 2010a. Report on the Twenty Ninth Meeting of the Council of Ministers. Theme: Harnessing Science and Technology for Development. Lusaka: COMESA

COMESA, 2010b. Trade Facilitation Study in COMESA: Pilot Case Study on COMESA Sub-region. Lusaka: COMESA

Draper, P. 2012. Competitiveness, Protectionism, and the WTO. Johannesburg: South Africa Institute of International Affairs.

Drew, S., Cox, S., and Warr, D. 2014. Guideline for Ethical Visual Research Methods. Melbourne: University of Melbourne.

Drope, J. 2011. Tobacco control in Africa: People Politics and Policies, London: Arithem Press.

Dube, C and Ngoma, S. 2012. Aid for Trade and Economic Development : A Case Study of Zambia. Lusaka: CUTS international.

Kalungia, K.S. 2001. Impact of Small Scale Cross-border Trade in Eastern and Southern Africa. Lusaka: Regional Integration Research Network.

Mambara, J.L. 2007. COMESA Customs Union: An Assessment for Progress and Challenges for Eastern and Southern Africa's poor. Harare: Trade and Development Studies centre.

Sukume, E.E., Makudze, R.M., Chimedza, M and Zitsana, N. 2000. Comparative Advantage of Crop Production in Zimbabwe. Harare: USAID Publications.

Zhou, G. 2006. An Analysis of the Objectives and Effects of Privatisation on the Private Sector Role of the State in Zimbabwe. Harare: Zimbabwe Coalition on Debt and Development.

CHAPTER THREE

Border Management Systems' Intelligence and Annotations on Existing Transit Challenges in Zimbabwe.

Felistas R Zimano, Donald Chimanikire and Alouis Chilunjika

Introduction

Existing Border Management Systems (BMS) present challenges and opportunities to countries in their individual capacities as well as in their various groupings. These BMS include, both, on and off-site logistics related to the passage of people and cargo across countries' borders. BMS also includes the hard and soft infrastructure components that go into the passage of people and cargo across countries' territorial boundaries. The challenges and opportunities differ in extent from country to country. The border, being the entry and exit point for a country, is the playground for a myriad of human and cargo movements related problems and opportunities. These challenges and opportunities have crosscutting implications on the country's security facets (be it economic, environmental, social, political, ecological security etc).

For all known border related challenges, various initiatives have been rolled out across the world with varying degrees of success. It is against that background that this chapter seeks to present some of the initiatives being used in various parts of the world. This chapter does not aim to recommend these initiatives to any country. The aim is to expose policymakers to what others are doing. This can serve as their learning and reference tool. In the opinion of the authors, there are times when local policymakers seem to be surrendering the occurrence of some incidents to fate. These are times when, from the scholars' point of view, policymakers' deportment shows that some problems do not have solutions. Whilst policymakers will be saying, 'we are looking into it,' evidence on the ground will be showing that they are thinking, 'this problem does not have a solution'. This demonstrates a clear case of lack of innovation spirit and risk-taking which should be part of solution hunting. Such is the case with most border related challenges in less-developed countries. On a lot of forums, as evidenced by various newspaper reports, issues of smuggling, human trafficking, transit fraud, border delays and counterproductive demurrage are presented as undesirable things that are, inevitably, part of every border system. Policymakers seem to accept these problems as part and parcel of normal border operations. It is no wonder why at every World Trade Organisation (WTO) meeting the issue of trade facilitation is always a hot one between more-developed and less-developed countries. Less-developed countries are seen to be going against the core principles of WTO on trade. In some circles corruption by customs official has been christened 'facilitation fee'. It has become an acceptable 'token' paid in order to hasten the clearance process. This is a sign of desperation in its extreme sense as even business people get to incorporate such unjustified expenses into their cost of doing business plans.

However, some countries have made significant strides in eliminating and reducing most border related challenges by continuously transforming their BMS. The secret to their success lies evidently in research, adaptability, responsiveness and sincerity in tackling border related challenges. According to PWC (2015:7) "innovative technology and infrastructure, effective international cooperation, coherent processes and an agile organisation" constitute the best approach to BMS. A lot of solutions are lying out there but there is apparent lack of insight into what is obtaining in other parts of the world. On international forums, the developing countries have armed themselves to defend their failure by arguing that they are not acting up to standards and WTO core principles because developing countries are reluctant to pay for the trade adjustment costs in developing countries.

Depressingly, there are also local policymakers who do not know what is obtaining on various border points under their jurisdiction as most prefer, and have limited themselves to, air transport to road transport. The policymakers, as such, live in their own world yet they are expected to deliver for the problems on the ground. The other critical issue is the lack of highly educated professional bureaucracy to bring in analytical skills relevant for sound policy prescriptions. This chapter brings together measures put in place in various parts of the world as well as documented challenges from the Zimbabwean case for use by policymakers as reference point. Policymakers from other parts of Southern Africa, in search of solutions, can also relate this work to their specific problems and come out with customised or hybrid solutions. It is only through well-thought solutions that their problems can be addressed in their peculiarity. With such initiatives and sincere implementation, a lot of border related challenges experienced in most developing countries can be reduced or even eliminated.

Methodology

A single case study is developed herein through electronic literature review. The researchers purposively singled out Zimbabwe as it is their home country. Besides being a familiar territory in which lived experiences inform their arguments, they wrote with an aim to contribute to its development. The Zimbabwean case is taken to illustrate problems faced due to shortcomings in the existing BMS. The single case study is preferred in this because of its strengths relevant to this BMS study. Single case study has a better ability to help create more complicated theories on one hand whilst on the other it can be generalised to other single cases (Mariotto, Zanni and De Moraes, 2014). Single case also "offers rich data for in-depth analysis and understanding of issues in their natural life context" (Gaya and Smith, 2016, p. 529). Once the Zimbabwean case is presented, a presentation of intelligence on existing BMS from literature will trail. This will lead into the rest of the discussion, conclusions and recommendations. Two classes of literature are considered: newspapers and academic literature. The literature from electronic newspapers present border related challenges common in developing countries using the case of Zimbabwe. A snapshot of select 2017 electronic newspaper reports on Zimbabwe borders' cases will be utilised in building the BMS case study. The use of 2017 cases is to show that border problems indeed persist on Zimbabwe's borders. Although this might not cover enough information like would be the case of a longitudinal study, it suffice to show that existing BMS' problems have been captured in recent media reports.

Border Management Systems (BMS) concept

BMS refers to a system with several constituent parts. BMS encompasses administrative networks, information systems and infrastructure for countries entry and exit points (Ferraro and De Capitani, 2016). As such, BMS build up to be everything that goes into the operations of border points. BMS consist of both hard and soft infrastructure used in the management of border points (Zimano and Ruffin, 2018). The infrastructure can be found, as will be discussed in forthcoming parts of this chapter, located on or off the border posts' sites. At border sites the usual infrastructure include holding bays, clearing bays, customs offices and machinery, weigh bridges, immigration offices and machinery among other things. However, some of these and more can be found off the border site. In some countries, for example in the Schengen arrangement, weigh bridges are not on the border sites. The innovations and advancements in technology have also seen a lot of customs and clearing administrative offices being located far from the border site. Technology has also helped countries revolutionise their BMS. Effective use of technology can enable governments to "track movements, secure identity and automate decision-making" (PWC, 2015). Varying levels of integration have also seen the total removal of several border processes in various parts of the world particularly in the Schengen area, named above, which has eased transit related challenges.

Broad as it is, the term BMS embraces all the nitty-gritty concerning passage of goods from one country to another in a very simplified manner. The bottom line is that BMS is measured on efficiency. On the legislation part, the BMS are generally the same for all modes of transport as people and cargo go through more or less the same clearance procedures when exiting or entering a country. However, a few variations will be found depending on the mode of transport as some regulations are specific. This is because, for example, whilst the type of goods and value permitted per individual will remain the same for all travellers, varying weight and goods type restrictions would apply for air, road, rail, sea and pipe modes of transport.

From the above outline, it is clear that BMS form the basis of various components of a country. BMS have implications to a country's performance in international trade as factors that affect the passage of goods through a country's borders affect the performance of a country's goods on the international market. BMS also affects a country's political security as the systems in use at borders help to curb illegal movement of people and cargo. Economically, BMS contribute to a country's revenue collection abilities with weak BMS resulting in revenue leakages. In short, BMS plays a role in every facet of economic, social, political, ecological and security performance of a country. More on BMS and challenges will be exposed in the forthcoming sections 4 and 5 as literature review.

The literature for this chapter is in two parts. The first part is tabulated literature showing snapshot of the border related challenges rife in Zimbabwe; a case from Southern Africa. All these electronic newspaper stories were reported in the year 2017. This will be followed by a presentation of various measures that build into BMS being used in other parts of the world to curb various border related challenges.

Endemic Border related challenges in Southern Africa: the Zimbabwean case

Table 1. 2017 Electronic Newspapers' literature on Zimbabwe borders' challenges

Challenge	Headline and source URL	Story highlights
Transit fraud	Government must act on transit fraud. http://www.chronicle.co.zw/government-must-act-on-transit-fraud/ 2017, March 10.	-restricted goods getting into Zimbabwe under transit banner -rife abuse of travellers' rebate -tankers moving fuel purported for transit, offloading in

		Zimbabwe and refilling with water.
Smuggling	Smuggling distressing business. https://www.newsday.co.zw/2017/03/smuggling-distressing-business/ 2017, March 30.	-goods smuggled sold at lower price on illegal market -some smuggled goods finding way into big retail markets shelves -Textile and cement industry suffering from cheap illegal imports
Corruption	Long queues resurface at border posts. https://www.newsday.co.zw/2017/12/long-queues-resurface-border-posts/ 2017, December 18.	-long queues at Plumtree and Beitbridge -delays blamed on system sabotage

| Delays | Volume of traffic increases at Beitbridge border posts

https://www.herald.co.zw/volume-of-traffic-increases-at-beitbridge-border-post/

2017, December 25. | -travellers and transporters spending six to nine hours to be cleared.

-congestion due to unavailability of infrastructure to accommodate surging volumes of traffic.

-travellers cleared in good time still had to wait as their buses and vehicles took longer to be cleared

-system failing to deal with seasonal surge in travellers characterising festive season. |
| Weak information technology (IT) systems | Massive traffic cripples Zim borders... ZIMRA blames IT outage for chaos

https://www.dailynews.co.zw/articles/2017/12/21/massive-traffic-cripples-zim-borders-zimra-blames-it-outage-for-chaos | -chaos traced to computer system outage

-ZIMRA experienced challenges |

	2017, December 21.	with the Automated Systems for Customs Data (ASYCUDA) -long queues for both travellers and transporters
Lack of sincere implementati on	One stop border project abandoned. http://www.financialgazette.co.zw/one-stop-border-project-abandoned/ 2017, October 19.	-officers reverting to the old clearance system -officers trained in the one-stop-border-posts system transferred to other stations, new personnel lack training. -clearance process slipped back to four days.

Sources: as inserted

Border Management Systems (BMS) intelligence in literature

There are a number of ways to alleviate challenges at entry-points, some of which have been tried in different parts of the world while some are mere proposals in literature. The effectiveness of the methods varies from situation to situation due to many other intervening factors. In most cases, these methods are used in combination for better results.

Some of the methods are also already in use in Zimbabwe, the case under study, and the rest of Southern Africa. However, the continued incidences of border related challenges justify the need for more research. This can be used to evaluate and improve what subsist on the ground.

Transit corridors and Computer based risk-management systems

The level of performance in international trade for countries depends on the costs of doing business incurred in their production lines and government taxes (Zimano, 2017). One of the major components in costs is transit costs. Landlocked countries suffer more on transit charges as compared to their coastal counterparts. Initiatives to alleviate transits costs for landlocked countries can come in the form of transit corridors. According to Jain (2012:66), putting in place regulations for the movement of goods across other countries' territorial areas that do not have flaws is crucial for those countries that do not have coastal borders, as it ensures that the cost of moving goods is kept to a minimum. Practical solutions such as corridors for the movement of goods across several countries, and the coming together of countries in a region to work together and change some key policies, can go a long way to lessening the impact of being landlocked (Hewitt and Gillson, 2003:77). Transit corridors can ease movement problems as they expand the existing infrastructure and also increase the capacity of transport networks. This will aid in speeding up the time taken to deliver goods. However, "every border infrastructure investment should follow a comprehensive re-engineering of systems and procedures, and it should be designed specifically to support the adoption of modern border management" (Zarnowiecki, 2011:37).

Ghana's transit corridor initiative, for example, can be a learning point on how to alleviate border-related problems. The country's Economic Recovery Programme had, among several intentions, the desire to revive the country's economy. As part of that programme, Ghana adopted the Gateway Project (Bohene-Osafo, 2003:105), which included an initiative by the Ministry of Roads and Transport and the Ministry of Trade. The "Ghana Shippers Council, under the auspices of the Ministry of Roads and Transport, liaised with the shippers' councils in some of the landlocked countries in the sub-region to negotiate agreements that would facilitate the establishment of a transit corridor through Ghana to these countries" (Bohene-Osafo, 2003:105). This saw the Ministry taking up the task of improving the road network of the country.

In Ghana, over and above the transit corridor initiative, a computer-based Risk Management Systems (RMS) was also introduced to select imported goods for examination (Bohene-Osafo, 2003:108). As such, targets were established to significantly reduce the physical examinations of cargo (Bohene-Osafo, 2003:108). "Based on risk assessment, shipments are separated into three examination categories, namely, high risk (red channel); medium risk (yellow channel); and low risk (green channel)" (Bohene-Osafo, 2003:108). This sees goods getting priority clearance depending on their level of risk. Those goods with low risk will go to a channel where the inspection process is less rigorous than the other two categories, which is a step towards ensuring that measures and inspection infrastructure can be customised depending on the level of risk of a shipment.

Multiple initiatives legislation

Multiple initiatives legislation is a necessary instrument for the operations of the transit corridors mentioned above. In 1999, six Asian countries set out and signed an agreement regulating their trade (Barka, 2012:10). This was a very complex initiative with a lot of proposals. This included regularising the procedures for people moving across borders, such that they ended up having similar standards and measures (Barka, 2012:10). This culminated in Joint Customs Controls at border sites that were identified for the programme (Barka, 2012:10).

Such initiatives go a long way in ensuring systems interface and standardisation. Lack of systems interface is the main reason for duplication of roles and delays experienced at most border entry and exit points. The absence of such overarching legislation also leads to the multiplicity of players at entry points. Therefore, coming up with legislation to allow joint controls will ensure the elimination of duplicity, unnecessary delays and the number of players at border points. This will enhance the flow of goods. If coupled with a transit corridor, such initiatives will complement each other and drastically reduce the cost of doing business for landlocked countries.

Pre-shipment inspection (PSI), Tamperproof sealing and Global Positioning System (GPS) tracking

These three initiatives work jointly, as such, will be discussed simultaneously in this part. To curb corruption at borders, some countries have implemented a PSI. This is a practice in which private companies check details of shipments "such as price, quantity and quality of goods" before they are dispatched, to help 'compensate for inadequacies in administrative infrastructures' (WTO Publication n.d.).This entails carrying out inspection procedures to check compliance to the set regulations before goods are exported (Hewitt and Gillson, 2003:78). This practice of inspecting before exporting helps to curb the loss of revenue through customs fraud, such as the undervaluing of goods, classifying goods in a way that will make them appear in an incorrect category so that they pay less taxes, and several other related issues (Hewitt and Gillson, 2003:78). This lessens the burden on the border, as instead of going through all the inspections, the border authorities just check that the tamperproof seal installed after the PSI has not been broken. This goes a long way in easing traffic delays at the entry points.

Tamperproof sealing of containers is a system in which cargo is inspected and sealed at point of origin. These inspections would be done by responsible parties away from the border, where the consignment will be originating from. Once this is done, the containers will be sealed with all parties in agreement. Containers that have tamperproof sealing will help to ensure that the cargo reaches its destination securely (Hufbauer and Schott, 2005:17). This method is envisioned to lessen the strain at the borders significantly. Once trucks are inspected with both parties in agreement, an express route would be used that would mean there would be very minimal delay. At most, the clearance that will be needed at the border is that for the driver only. Non-invasive inspection can then be done using technical scanners that can detect illicit goods without having to physically open and inspect cargo at entry and exit points (PWC, 2015).

The GPS then comes in handy through remote monitoring to help tracking location of goods. GPS helps to bring accountability on demurrage as some transporters have been fingered in creation of false delays to ensure they charge organisations more in demurrage costs. GPS provides, among other things; directions, navigation, timing operations precision and offender monitoring (Milner, 2016). Once stoppage is detected on the GPS, organisations can know where exactly the challenges will be and call for interventions accordingly. Surveillance drones and infrared cameras can also be incorporated to ensure efficiency (PWC, 2015)

Cashless systems at borders and Biometric scanning

Another source of delays and corruption at entry points is the multiple cashier systems dealing with physical cash. Most people will agree that borders have also become a haven of people exchanging currencies illegally due to the continued use of cash for most payments. One way to curb such practices and associated delays will be through the introduction of cashless systems at border entry and exit points. When it comes to dealing with corruption, a case from the Philippines gives some insights. According to Ndonga (2013:30), "customs reform in the Philippines started in 1992 with the election of President Fidel Ramos". Among other things, the president called for the restoration of "sanity" in customs, which led to the introduction of reform programmes (Ndonga, 2013:30). The Philippines reforms culminated in severe re-engineering of the key customs processes. Among other things, the system was automated and a "cashless" system adopted. "This new cashless system ensured that customs cashiers did not get an opportunity to abscond with their cash collections," (Ndonga, 2013:30). Ultimately, "the introduction of the various systems played a key role in reducing the extensive discretionary interfaces that customs officials enjoyed and consistently manipulated for their personal gain" (Ndonga, 2013, 30).

Such an initiative helps both the government and the transacting public. Cashless system plug off revenue leakages. This improves the government's revenue collection system. Secondly, the transacting public can make payments remotely then go on to present proof of payments to the inspectors. This can significantly reduce delays at entry points. A complementary initiative to support cashless system is the biometric scanning. Biometric system is a real-time method of identification and individuals' verification in which person specific characteristics are scanned for security purposes (Jeddy, Radhika and Nithya, 2017). Of late, biometrics are being linked to digital identities linked to several sectors effectively creating a powerful 'ecosystem' of identity information with a highly reduced error rates (Dixon, 2017). As such, biometrics and cashless systems can be linked and effectively eliminate the less reliable paper system. In Aruba, an island in the Caribbean Sea, a model biometric technology and modern passport scanning system is in place which also provides extensive information on tourism (PWC, 2015).

Once systems have been made cashless and biometric scanning is in place, countries will have made significant strides towards eliminating the physical handling of transactions at borders which go a long way in reducing corruption. An advanced model in use is the 'Smart Borders Package' being rolled out in the Schengen area. This is an electronic system which records travellers for automated verification (PWC, 2015). This system is envisaged to be fully implemented in the Schengen area by 2020.

One Stop Border Posts (OSBP), Juxtaposed offices and coordinated border management

Delays at border posts can also be traced to the requirement to clear goods separately on exit and entry points. OSBP and juxtaposed offices are initiatives that have been adopted to ease such challenges. The use of the OSBP system is new to SADC; the Chirundu OSBP project pioneered the concept in Sub Saharan Africa (Kassee, 2014:105). Under an OSBP adjoining countries agree to honour clearance in either country for both exit and entrance. This means once traffic is cleared for exit, as an example, on either of the two countries, it will not need to stop again in the adjoining country to go through entrance formalities. Before the establishment of the OSBP at Chirundu, trucks and travellers went through lengthy clearance times at each entry point that could take as long as five days. Since the introduction of the OSBP system clearance is done within a day, with the number of trucks being cleared averaging 480 per day (Kassee, 2014, p. 105). This means that tangible benefits are present. However, recent evidence from electronic newspapers presented in the foregoing section shows that authorities are reneging on the implementation of the OSBP system at Chirundu. This has seen the coming back of queues as gains brought by the OSBP are eroded.

Another arrangement is one between Switzerland and France, that is, "juxtaposed offices". In this arrangement an agreement at the bilateral level was adopted, in which countries sharing borders with Switzerland were co-opted so that their officers could be legalised to work in another state in offices specifically designed to deal with movement of goods and people and their subsequent clearance (Polner, 2011:58). This arrangement saw exporters from France accessing customs clearance in Switzerland, that is, they were given clearance services for export and import documentation under one roof. This arrangement reduces border delays because commercial fleets do not have to stop twice for clearance. The arrangement of juxtaposed facilities comes in two forms; in addition to the one explained above, there can be an arrangement in which two countries merge their processes (Zarnowiecki, 2011:64).

The use of coordinated border management is another measure espoused to ease the movement of goods and people. This can be done in two approaches. The first, according to Jain (2012:65), is to aid the movement of goods by using a system that is created to ensure that agencies communicate information among themselves. This will reduce the repetition that is common in processing. This works well when the parties are involved under a combined arrangement that takes care of all the agencies' plights (Jain, 2012:65). The second approach is coordinated border management, which brings together countries sharing borders to work together in order to reduce the repetitions that come with doing the procedures independently (Jain, 2012:65). This requires good inter-agency coordination. Coordination at country levels is coming with the realisation that security problems have now grown beyond the capacity of individual countries (PWC, 2015).

Customs regulations and infrastructure reforms

Some challenges in the existing BMS in use can be traced to the archaic nature of systems in use. Some systems are so out-dated that they are no longer relevant for the security and speed demands of this era. Situations where physical flagging of vehicles to stop being done manually practiced in some border posts is one example of an out-dated and inefficient system being used to date. There is also a challenge whereby the soft and hard infrastructure at border points are not compatible due to the latter being out-dated. To avoid this, there is need to link the soft and hard infrastructure at border points as there is evident marriage between the two (Zimano and Ruffin, 2018). Failure to establish a link between hard and soft infrastructure has attributed to incidences in which, at some point, the Chirundu OSBP was by legislation a OSBP yet in practice operated as a two-stop-border-post. Such occurrences mean the advantages that should be enjoyed from it being a OSBP are eroded as the soft infrastructure will not be communicating properly with the hard infrastructure.

In Afghanistan, a programme for reforming the customs systems was initiated in 2004 with some input from the World Bank. The programme was focused on "infrastructure improvement, automation of customs procedures, clarifying and reforming the roles and responsibilities of the various government agencies operating at the border" (McLinden and Durrani, 2013:7). This produced very good results. "Revenue collection increased (from USD77 million in 2003-04 to more than USD900 million in 2009-10) and truck release times decreased substantially (for Kabul ICD from 428 minutes for Customs in 2003 to 277 minutes in 2006). At border stations such as Torkham and Hairatan, truck release time fell to 39 and 26 minutes respectively (from an average time of almost a day or more)" (McLinden and Durran, 2013:7). However, despite these reforms, corruption has remained rife in the Afghanistan system. This shows that there is a need for more concerted efforts across the system, as some of the causes may be deeply ingrained into the government structures and people's culture.

Collaborative border management

A measure that has been termed "collaborative border management" is also espoused in the literature. According to Doyle (2011:11), the collaborative management of borders is rooted in the formulation of proper guidelines for the regulation of the interactions of the business and government communities, throughout the supply chain that goods pass through from the producer to the end user. This is a scenario whereby the issues to do with the management of the border are developed in consultation with all the involved players, both public and private. Collaborative border management has benefits for both the government and the private players. In this arrangement an imaginary border inspects goods, qualifying some to proceed across the border and disqualifying those that do not meet the regulations long before the goods get to the actual border (Doyle, 2011:14). Such arrangements are very much advanced in New Zealand. This means that agencies have to work together and share information. Ordinarily, this sharing of information will go a long way to reducing duplications and unnecessary delays. However, this collaborative border management system is not arrived at through forced organisational change. It "requires strong political will and commitment and appropriate incentives and disincentives" (Doyle, 2011:14). This system has a lot of benefits, as shown in Table 2.

Table 2: Collaborative border management benefits

Benefits to the government	Benefits to the private sector
Lowering of overall costs of border management	Cutting costs through reducing delays and informal payments
Enhancing security. This extends to supply chain security	Enabling faster clearance and release
Improving intelligence and enforcement	Explaining rules, making their application more predictable and consistent
Increased trade compliance	Reduced unforeseen supply interruptions
Allowing the more effective and efficient deployment of resources	
Increasing integrity and transparency	
Accurate and improved revenue yield with less leakage	

Source: Doyle (2011:110 and Li (2011:86)

The last three items on the table above show benefits that accrue to both sectors in a similar way. These are benefits like increased integrity and transparency. This means that collaborative border management has some benefits that are specific to the government, others specific to the private sector and some benefits can be attributed to both. Clear steps are needed to arrive at the collaborative border management indicated above. These steps start from the creation of a vision to that stage when stakeholders define the process and determine capacity.

Table 3: Transformation considerations for collaborative border management

Step	Action	Explanation
1.	Creating a vision	-A simple vision understandable to all needs to be developed and owned by all stakeholders -It need to be seen as a win for all participants
2.	Establishing leadership and governance	-Leadership at each border management agency must agree to the vision and commit to delivering the agreed business outcomes -Leadership needs a mandate from government -A governance structure is needed to direct and monitor performance -Create a common mission
3.	Making the business case	-The case for change needs to be approved -A clear vision with associated business outcomes can start this process -Governments, and all the stakeholders that interact with border management agencies, need to understand the benefits of collaborative border management
4.	Conducting diagnostic assessment	-An agency's current position must be assessed against its target position -Lessons from within and outside the country should be incorporated

5.	Defining processes and determining capabilities	-Mapping all the key processes associated with collaborative border management promotes seamless integration
		-Can reveal duplications and redundancies in business operations, identify best practices, and distinguish between core and non-core processes
		-A well designed capability assessment should focus on operations efficiency and having a knowledgeable, skilled and motivated workforce in the right place and right time

Source: Doyle (2011, p. 17-18)

Once the above listed actions are put in place, a collaborative border management system can be established. This is just one of the several ways of modernising existing BMS that can help transform the Southern Africa transit regime.

Getting to modern BMS - Notes for policymakers

The border related challenges obtaining in Southern Africa as amplified by the Zimbabwean case are inimical to business. There is need to find ways to address these problems. From the intelligence presented above, there are several ways to bring about the desired modern BMS. The bottom line is that people want transit efficiency. This is critical because everything that happens in transit builds into the trade transaction costs (Zimano and Ruffin, 2018). Foremost, policymakers need to get out of their offices and accustom themselves to what is obtaining on the ground. A scenario whereby most policymakers are not consumers of the products they purport to represent is disheartening. Policymakers in BMS must get first-hand experience by alternating and using all modes of transport to travel in and out of their countries. A situation in which most policymakers are confined to using air transport is inimical to their understanding of the situation obtaining on road entry and exit border points.

There is evidence that several initiatives have been put in place in trying to improve existing BMS. However, as presented above, challenges persist. The existence of transit fraud and smuggling has been reported as linked to the scenario in which prohibited goods flood local markets. Cases have also been cited in which fuel smuggling takes place with transporters offloading in countries like Zimbabwe before proceeding to their destination with containers filled with water. This is a challenge that can be addressed through the tamperproof and GPS system presented above. Once a vehicle in transit has been cleared as such, tracking devices can be activated so that detours and stoppages are closely monitored to ensure that goods are not dumped in the wrong country.

The other rot at entry and exit points exposed in electronic newspapers is corruption and delays. These have been linked, in some cases to the human factor. The personnel manning border points have been cited as manipulating the systems in order to create artificial delays. These artificial delays will force people to give into the personnel's' corrupt demands through payments of 'facilitation fees'. Such practices can be curbed through installation of CCTV cameras and under cover inspection personnel. Those found wanting should be relieved of their duties. Reports in media shows that this has happened before but this should not be a once off exercise. Personnel manning border points must always be kept under check if these delays are to be curbed. Such sabotage should not be tolerated as it has dire consequences on the general image of a country as well as negative downstream effects on the cost of doing business.

Closely related to the point on personnel above, there have been reports on weak IT systems and feeble implementation of the OSBP system at Chirundu. Whilst the personnel have been fingered as tampering with the IT systems to create artificial delays, the weakness also lies with the IT system in place. Governments must always endeavour to invest in best IT systems with credible backup systems. On implementation of the OSBP, reports indicate that the moment when the trained personnel were transferred to other stations, the implementation of the OSBP system stalled. This is because the replacement personnel were not properly trained for the system. This clearly shows lack of planning and insincerity on the part of the management. Governments need to put in place proper monitoring programmes to ensure that support systems are always in place for the proper implementation of existing legislation and utilisation of infrastructure. Cases in which OSBP system operates as a TSBP system as reported in media erode all the benefits that come with modern BMS.

The issue of long queues and congestion can be dealt with by almost all the BMS initiatives listed above. The need to ensure the hard and soft infrastructure complement each other cannot be overemphasized. Adopting PSI, tamper proofing and GPS tracking can help decongest the border areas. There will be no need for having such facilities as weigh bridges and truck holding bays in the border areas. Routes for pre-cleared traffic can be created and most business people are likely to embrace such initiatives as they can make proper planning for their business once unnecessary demurrage is reduced. To cap it all, strides towards making all the border points transactions paperless must be initiated. This comes through the introduction of cashless payment platforms and the biometric systems.

Conclusion

This chapter puts existing intelligence on BMS in one place. Without brushing away efforts made so far, transit challenges persist in Southern Africa as evidenced by the Zimbabwean case. The Zimbabwean challenges chronicled in this chapter, from 2017 electronic newspaper sources, show the extent to which the challenges still stick with the region regardless of efforts made and muted through implementation of OSBP, several transit corridor projects and IT systems. At the same time, the chapter has shown that the human factor also plays a pivotal role in the effective transformation towards modernising of existing BMS. With sincerity and cooperation, these challenges will pass. Policy makers need to commit to the transformation and continued improvement of BMS as transit logistical costs feed into trade facilitation by offering opportunities and challenges to the cost of doing business. Once this is done, less-developed countries' advantageous participation in international trade will be on course. On top of all these initiatives, policymakers need to get exposed to the existing BMS in use in their countries. They should get out of their offices and be on the ground in order to get first-hand information on obtains in areas under their jurisdiction.

References

Bohene-Osafo, C. 2003. Enhancing Trade and Transport Facilitation in Africa, in: Developing Countries in United Nations Economic Commision for Europe. Sharing the Gains of Globalization in the New Security Environment. New York: United Nations, pp. 105-114.

Dixon, P. 2017. A Failure to "Do No-Harm" – India's Aadhaar Biometric ID Program and its Ability to Protect Privacy in Relation to Measures in Europe and the US. Health Technol. Vol. 7, No. 4, pp. 539-567.

Doyle, T. 2011. The Future of Border Management, in: McLinden, G., Fanta, E., Widdowson, D., et al.(eds), Border Management Moderniz ation, Washington: The World Bank, pp. 11-22.

Gaya, H. J and Smith, E. E. 2016. Developing a Qualitative Single Case Study in the Strategic Management Realm: An appropriate Research Design? International Journal for Business Management and Econo mic Research. Vol. 7, No. 2, pp. 529-538.

Hewitt, A., and Gillson, I. 2003. Income Distribution Impact of Trade Facilitation in Developing Countries, in: UNECFE, Sharing the Gains of Globalisation in the New Security Environment: The Challenges to Trade Facilitation, New York: United Nations, pp. 73-104.

Hufbauer, G. C., and Schott, J. J. 2005. NAFTA Revisited. Achievements and Challenges,Washington DC: Institute for International Economics.

Jain, S. R. 2012. Coordinated Border Management: The Experience of Asia and the Pacific Region, World Customs Journal, 6 (1), pp. 63-74.

Jeddy, J., Radhika, T and Nithya, S. 2017. Tongue Prints in Biometric Authentication: A Pilot Study. Journal of Oral and Maxillofacial Pathology. Vol. 21, No. 1, pp. 176-179.

Li, Y., McLinden, G., and Wilson, J. S. 2011. 'Building a Convincing Business Case for Border management reform, in: McLinden, G., Fanta, E., Widdowson, D., et al.(eds), Border Management Mordenization, Washington DC: The World Bank, pp. 79-94.

Mariotto, F. L., Zanni, P. P and De Moraes, G. H. S. M. 2014. What is the use of a Single Case Study in Management Research? Revista de Administração de Empresas, Vol. 54, No. 4, pp. 358-369.

McLinden, G., and Durrani, A. Z. 2013. Corruption in Customs,World Customs Journal, 7 (2), pp. 3-9.

Milner, G. 2016. What is GPS? Journal of Technology in Human Services. Vol. 34, No. 1, pp. 9-12.

Ndonga, D. 2013. Managing the Risk of Corruption in Customs Through The Single Window Systems,World Customs Journal,7 (2), pp. 23-37.

Polner, M. 2011. Coordinated Border Management: From Theory to Practice, World Customs Journal, 5 (2), pp. 49-64.

Zarnowiecki, M. 2011. Borders, Their design and Their Operation,in: McLinden, G., Fanta, E., Widdowson, D., et al. (eds), Border Management Modernization, Washington DC: The World Bank, pp. 37-78.

Zimano F. R. 2017. 'Road Entry Point Management Systems and Region al Integration: The Case of Zimbabwe'. Unpublished Thesis. Universi ty of KwaZulu Natal

Zimano, F. R and Ruffin, F. 2018. Palpable linkage of Supply Chain Management to Hard and Soft Infrastructure Marriage: The Case of SADC Road Entry Point Management Systems. International Journal of Logistics Systems and Management (forthcoming).

Online Sources

Barka, H, B. 2012. Border Posts, Checkpoints and Intra African Trade Challenges and Solutions.[Online]. Available at :http://www.afdb.org /fileadmin/uploads/afdb/Documents/Publications/INTRA%20AF RICAN%20TRADE_INTRA%20AFRICAN%20TRADE.pdf [Accessed 14 February, 2015]

Ferraro, F and De Capitani, E. 2016. The New European Border and Coast Guard: Yet another "halfway" EU reform? European Research Academy. [Online]. Available at http://www.sipotra.it/wp content/u ploads/2017/02/The-new-European-Border-and-Coast-Guard-yet-another-%E2%80%9Chalf-way%E2%80%9D-EU-reform.pdf [Accessed 20 February, 2018]

Mashaya, B. 2017, December 21. Massive Traffic Cripples Zim Borders – ZIMRA Blames IT Outage for Chaos. Daily News [Online] Available at https://www.dailynews.co.zw/articles/2017/12/21/massive traffi c-cripples-zim-borders-zimra-blames-it-outage-for-chaos [Accessed 10 February, 2018]

Muleya, T. 2017, December 25. Volume of Traffic Increases at Beitbridge Border Post.Herald. [Online] Available at https://www.he rald.co.zw/volume-of-traffic-increases-at-beitbridge-border-post/ [Accessed 10 February, 2018]

Muleya, T. 2017, March 10. Government must act on Transit Fraud. Chronicle. [Online] Available at http://www.chronicle.co.zw/govern ment-must-act-on-transit-fraud/ [Accessed 20 February, 2018]

Nyoni, M. 2017, March 30. Smuggling Distressing Business.Newsday. [Online] Available at https://www.newsday.co.zw/2017/03/smuggli ng-distressing-business/ [Accessed 20 February, 2018]

PWC.2015. The Future of Border Management: Mantaining Security. Facilitating Prosperity, Public Safety and Justice Publications. [Online] Available at https://www.pwc.com/m1/en/publications/documents/the-future-of-border-management.pdf [Accessed 15 July, 2017].

Unnamed Correspondent.2017, December 18. Long Queues Resurface at Border Posts.Newsday. [Online] Available at https://www.newsday.c o.zw/2017/12/long-queues-resurface-border-posts/ [Accessed 10 Ferbuary, 2018]

Unnamed Correspondent. 2017, October 19. One Stop Border Project Abandoned. Financial Gazette. [Online] Available at (http://www.fin ancialgazette.co.zw/one-stop-border-project-abandoned/ [Accessed 1 February, 2018]

WTO Publication. 2014. [Online]. Available at: https://www.wto.org/en glish/tratop_e/preship_e/preship_e.htm [Accessed 20 December 2014].

CHAPTER FOUR

The Spatial and Physical Planning Considerationsand Implications on Border Management in Zimbabwe

Innocent Chirisa and Abraham Rajab Matamanda

Introduction and Background

Borders, borderlands, boundaries or frontiers refer to human creations grounded in various ethical traditions such as the need to demarcate and protect certain spatial territories and the subjects residing therein (Anderson, 1996; Weber, 2012). From time immemorial, these borders have been in existence as either 'artificial' human creation, for example, the border between South Africa and Namibia. In the Holy Bible, the story of the walls of Jericho is narrated in Joshua 6: 1-27. This story (walls of Jericho) is an indication of the existence of borders earlier in human history. These walls acted as a barrier of border which marked the territory of the inhabitants of the city. The Roman Empire also had boundaries at different levels within the city boundaries and these determined where different classes would reside, areas of recreation, and so on. (Anderson, 1996). The Great Wall of China is another remarkable physical barrier which demarcated the boundary of the country, and also helped in protecting the nation (Jing, 2015). On the other hand, borders may be established where humans cannot settle, so much that the natural landscape (rivers, mountains, etc.) end up becoming borders between different States. For example, the Argun River demarcates the Sino-Russian boundary (Mancini, 2013). Therefore, the existence of borders to mark and protect territories is a global phenomenon which has been there since time immemorial.

In the recent millennia, borders have taken on different dimensions as there are increasing complexities around the borders. Various scholars have focused on the trans-frontier border issues in relation to natural resources management with special focus on wildlife management

(Trouwborst *et al.*, 2016). Increasing security threats along borderlands are being exacerbated through terrorism, civil wars, human trafficking and public health issues as well as wildlife diseases such as anthrax and foot and mouth (Rodríguez-Saldaña, 2005; Attree *et al.*, 2014; Jakwa, 2017). Although artificial borders have been established to demarcate State boundaries, there are various geo-physical issues which ultimately complicate the planning and management of borderlands (Mancini, 2013). The main essence in planning is centred on the creation of human settlements which are safe, resilient, inclusive and ultimately contribute towards human well-being (United Nations, 2016). This means that regardless of the location, the physical environment has to be managed in a holistic way. However, events on the ground show that there seem to be a dearth of studies relating to the physical and spatial planning considerations and implications of border management in Zimbabwe.

Colonial rule in Africa resulted in the struggle for territory which compelled the colonial masters to draw boundaries marking and safeguarding their newly found territories. The constant threat of wars and the need to protect certain valued territory meant that the physiology of the state forced leaders to place particular emphasis on control of remote areas that were vulnerable, and could be lost easily in battle (Herbst, 2000). Considering that no single State could exist in isolation, there was need for certain entry and exit points which linked these fortified territories. This was mainly through road networks which stretched through different countries as well as water courses, the result was that settlements usually emerged at these entry/exit points, and these settlements are referred to in this chapter as Border Towns. However, an interesting point to note with border towns in most African countries, Zimbabwe included is the manner in which the boundaries were established by the colonial masters (Nkiwane, 1993).

Zimbabwe, like most African states was fortified during the colonial era resulting in the emergence of a border demarcating the country. It is argued that the boundaries of many countries, particularly but by no means exclusively in French-speaking Africa, were arbitrarily drawn by the colonial powers and were not encouraging frameworks of unified, legitimate, and capable states (Jackson and Rosberg, 1985: 46). On the other hand, Bentsi-Enchill (1976) points out that:

...the nineteenth century partition of Africa by the European colonial powers was not made with any intention to the boundaries of these traditional polities … the newly independent African states, are, in general, territorially composite and have inherent problems of domestic boundary demarcation and maintenance between the traditional polities and jurisdictions of which they are composed.

Ironically, these boundaries have remained unchanged following the independence of most African states. It follows that the existing boundaries are a replica and legacy of the colonial demarcations which in most instances failed to account for local political, sociological, economic or ethnic factors (Herbst, 2000; Mancini, 2013: 3-4). An interesting case is the borders which enclose Lesotho and Swaziland within South Africa yet the socio-cultural setting of these territories is the same (Nkiwane, 1993: 69). Unlike in the past where movement of human was minimal owing to small populations and primitive transport systems, the recent millennia is characterised by the notion of globalisation and highly mobile citizens which makes borders very active just like the interior.

Moreover, technology has brought about different dimension of viewing and conceptualising these border spaces. Interestingly, the traditional sociological, geographical features (for example, shared water courses and natural resources such as wild life) and ethnic factors have been difficult to domesticate simply through demarcating borders. Other issues to consider also in relation to the borders include the issue of health which is very critical if one considers how the fluid nature of the borders in West Africa became the pathway for Ebola-infected patients in 2014 (Cook and Salaam-Blyther, 2014). Considering this complexity of borders, a lot of questions remain unanswered as to how best spatial and physical planning can be undertaken in border spaces with the view to promote and facilitate the lives and safety of communities living in these areas as well as the nation at large. In this vein, there is a need to examine the spatial and physical planning considerations and implications of border management in Zimbabwe because such an examination has the potential to increase the collective power of those within them by providing the potential for organisation and preventing the diffusion of effort and energy (Foltz, 1981: 39).

Methodology

This study is qualitative in nature and makes use of both primary and secondary data sources. Secondary data sources include the review of documents and archival materials such as maps for Zimbabwe which have been analysed.

Literature Review and Theoretical Framework

Although they demarcate territories, borders have always emerged as complex spaces which present States with various socio-economic, environmental and political opportunities as well as challenges. An interesting case to note is the United States-Mexico border which accommodates approximately 11.5 million people who reside in the 42 counties and 39 Mexican municipalities located along this border (Homedes and Ugalde, 2003). The planning and management of this border space, therefore, requires a lot of attention and care which can also help to inform spatial and physical planning considerations in borders across the world. The Horn of Africa also bears testimony to the dynamics and conflicts which arise along borders, especially when there are scarce resources in the region (Weber, 2012). The manner in which the borders are established emerge as the first point of call which usually present tensions among communities around these 'lines' (Herbst, 2000). This is especially true when the borders are demarcated without paying full attention to sociological, political and ethnicity considerations (Mancini, 2013: 4).

Traditionally, borderlands were fortified areas where human settlement was minimal. Only primitive communities developed in these areas which were usually considered as unsafe and inhabitable. Owing to the advent of globalisation, population increase and subsequent demand for land, there is increasing concentration of human in borderlands. In Europe and America, trans-frontier urban agglomerations have been established where city-regions housing millions of people concentrate along international borders. Examples of such urban agglomerations include the Strasbourg metropolitan area (French-German border), Basel-Mulhouse-Freiburg (Swiss-French-German border), Tijuana-San Diego (Mexican-U.S. border) and in Asia. All these city regions have populations which are at least 300 000 and close to 4 million for some. Planning considerations in such cases include taking note of housing needs, employment opportunities, markets and utilities for citizens on both sides of the border (Homedes and Ugalde, 2003). However, this is not always an easy task considering the socio-economic and political systems which prevail in the two different administrative regions/States. A typical example is harmonising infrastructure development along the US-Mexico borders where the two states different with regards their level of development, governance systems as well as the culture of the citizens.

Issues of security are of great concern in borderlands (Mancini, 2013; European Commission, 2014). It is for this reason that forts were established while in recent years some border towns have been established with the aim of monitoring movement of people and goods between two countries sharing a common border (Wiegand, 2011). Hence there is a need to factor in security issues in spatial and physical planning and management of human settlements along borders as well as border regions in general. This is so because cases in terrorism, wars and human trafficking are especially prominent in these regions (Mancini, 2013). Planning considerations must, therefore, integrate security issues so as to make borderlands safe to the residents as well as avoiding being potential threats to national security (Hensel, 1999). Traditionally, for example, the Great Wall of China, physical barriers helped to protect the interior through denying enemies access into their territories (Jing, 2015). This approach to planning and managing borders is still in use to this day where fences are erected to demarcate and restrict citizens and wildlife from accessing the other side of the border (Trouwborst *et al.*, 2016). Yet, fencing is a restrictive mechanism of managing border spaces which is usually characterised with conflicts as human find alternative and innovative ways to by-pass the fences. In the developed world, technology is increasingly being adopted as the panacea to managing security issues along borders.

Public health usually emerges as the major challenge which has to be addressed along borders. This is so because, although borders may exist, diseases do not respect borders (Gustavan, Sodahlon and Bush, 2016). Examples of diseases which have plagued communities around borders or which have exposed the fluidity of borders include outbreak of river blindness and Ebola virus in West Africa (Frieden and Damon, 2015; Gustavan *et al.*, 2016). Although borders exist between countries in this region, population movement tends to be unregulated owing to bilateral agreement which allow free movement of citizens between Liberia, Guinea and Sierra Leone (CDC, 2016). The incidence of outbreak of swine-flue in Asia also explains why diseases control and public health are critical in border management (Huang, 2010).

In efforts to address the environmental and public health issues along the US-Mexican border the Border Health commission was established in 2000 with a view to strengthen the system of border health information along the border (Carillo *et al.*, 2017). Such a bilateral commitment from both countries has been somehow effective in addressing environmental and public health issues along this border, though there are some challenges which are experienced along the way. Other efforts to control and eliminate diseases include adoption of cross-border collaboration creative models. Such a model has been used in West Africa where ministries of health and technical partners in Guinea, Cote d'Ivoire, Liberia and Sierra Leone met to discuss and resolve cross-border neglected tropical diseases (Gustavan *et al.*, 2016). It is argued that border health security is a critical area through which surveillance of disease outbreak and spread may be done (Huang, 2010).

Shared river basins also present a challenge along borders. The right to abstract water from the river, harvest fish, and dispose waste water often calls for integrated approaches through which riparian states have to engage in collaborative work aimed at facilitating sustainable use of the water resources. However, in practice it emerges that water courses are usually characterised with complexities which impact on border management. Countries usually adopt different mechanisms in relation to water use and management while some activities done in certain parts of the water course may negatively impact on the other state.

For example, nutrient loading may be prominent in one state than the other as has been the case along the Finish-Norwegian River Basin District where there is widespread contamination from metallurgy in Russia (The Finnish-Norwegian River Basin District [FNRBD], 2016). Moreover, the river basin is also characterised by different levels of harbour pollution and wastewater and sewage on the Finish side which accommodate 80 000 inhabitants as compared to the 20 000 on the Norwegian side of the 48 000km^2 river basin (FNRBD, 2016). The Israeli-Palestinian border is also characterised by some conflicts and disjointed use and management practices which date back to the early 1980s, where untreated waste water and sewerage flowed regularly toward Jerusalem (Fischhendler, Dinar and Kotz, 2011). However, an agreement was finally made to link the Palestinian sewage system to Jerusalem sewage network which helped to reduce pollution of the water course along the border (Fischhendler *et al.*, 2011).

In efforts to address the water related issues along the Tana, Neiden and Pasvik catchment areas in Finland and Norway, the two governments have developed the River Basin Management Plan which seeks to:

> ...summarise ecological and chemical status of water bodies, set environmental goals and form a base for local, regional and national catchments' activity, by holistically administering water resources (FNRBD, 2016).

Likewise, 3 200km Mexico-US also concerns water management issues which have resulted in the formulation of a number of bi-national water management treaties between the two countries (Maganda, 2012). The bi-national water management frameworks along borders must help to control and mitigate incidences of flooding, biodiversity loss and ensure that economic analysis of water uses are undertaken such that there is equal benefits on both sides of the river basins. Most fish and wildlife species do not recognise the artificial boundaries created by man. In most instances, these species tend to be migratory and cross national boundaries, while some of them even span continents. Examples of borders which include significant amount of wildlife include:

- US-Canada border which forms a boundary of at least 17 US and 8 Canadian designated conservation areas. There are various wildlife species which are found along this border all which have historically moved freely along the border and this free movement still remains vital.
- The US-Mexico border forms a boundary of at least even US and Three Mexican designated conservation areas which include wildlife refuges, national parks and biosphere reserves.

The complication is that states tend to erect physical barriers along the borders which usually restrict the free and natural movement of the wildlife. In this way, the wildlife is also restricted from accessing vital resources such as water which may be abundant on one state of the fence. Thus, there is need for recognising the needs of the wildlife as well as the communities who live adjacent to these sanctuaries who also need to benefit from the wildlife.

Discussion of Findings

Zimbabwe is a land-locked country. Just like most African states her borders were demarcated by the British who colonised the country from 1890 to 1980 when the country finally gained independence. Subsequently, these borders have been retained post 1980 and at the present moment, Zimbabwe shares its border with South Africa on the south, Mozambique to the east, Botswana to the west and Zambia to the north (Figure 1). Figure 1 shows that all parts of the country's borders are shared with South Africa, Mozambique, Zambia or Botswana. The perimeter of the Zimbabwean border is also habitat to a number of National Parks such as Gonarezhou as well as river basins which are shared with neighbouring countries (Figure 2). There are also a number of border towns which include Beitbridge, Mutare, Chirundu, Nyamapanda and Plumtree. Therefore, there is great need to understand the spatial and physical planning considerations along the country's border.

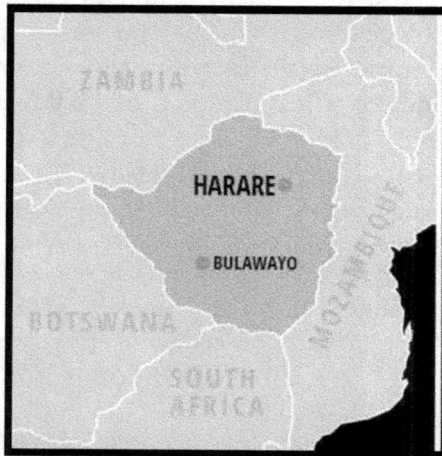

Figure 1: Zimbabwe and her neighbouring countries which she shares her borders with
Source:

The management of border towns in Zimbabwe is riddled with a plethora of socio-economic and environmental issues which compromise human well-being. The major challenge is infrastructure deficit which is typical of Chirundu town. Muqayi and Manyeruke (2015) highlighted that the Zimbabwean side of the Chirundu border does not have any health facility which results in citizens seeking medical services in Zambia. Housing challenges are also a challenge and this extends to other commercial services which fail to match the volume of travellers who pass through the town as well as those residing in the town (OECD, 2011). The unavailability of employment opportunities in the border towns leaves most citizens with little livelihood alternative. In the end, informality tends to be high as citizens seek to eke a living. Recently, citizens in Beitbridge have been complaining of increased crime and violence in the town which is mainly attributed to lack of employment opportunities in the town (Nyoni, 2018). Provision of basic services is also constrained in the borderlands.

Experiences from the US-Mexico, US-Canada and among other borders in Europe and America show that there are a lot of investments which are put in border towns with regard the provision of basic services, employment opportunities as well as infrastructure services. Although there are challenges associated with the approaches, for example, the cultural differences between Americans and Mexicans, every effort is made to ensure that there is good bi-national governance which recognises these differences and help in promoting liveable settlements where citizens do not feel the dichotomy but live as one community. The Israeli-Palestine situation where sewer pipes between the two countries have been connected with a view to contain waste water pollution is a good example of how some issues in service provision may be resolved along the borders.

Although associated with some problems such as spread of diseases, opening up borders and establishing a visa-free environment along the borders is critical as it helps in facilitating trade and commerce among the residents of the border towns who may find it difficult to access services from the neighbouring countries. A typical example is the case of Beitbridge border where residents from the Zimbabwean side get most of their basic commodities in Mussina which is approximately 20km from the Zimbabwe-South Africa border on the South African side. Such trade areas have been successfully established along the US-Canada, US-Mexico, Liberia-Sierra Leone and borders where they help in facilitating regional integration through trade and commerce. Markets are also established and sustained when the border towns are integrated. This is especially necessary in Chirundu where the Zimbabwean side is under-serviced and citizens on the Zimbabwean side depend on services from Lusaka which is closer by. The same is also true with regards infrastructural development such as clinics which may be shared between the two sides of the border.

There are two prominent river basins which are shared between Zimbabwe and other neighbouring countries. Zambezi River Basin is on the Zimbabwe-Zambia border. It is one of largest and is the most shared river basins in the SADC region. More than half of the 15 SADC member states have a stake in the Zambezi River Basin (SADC, 2015). The Limpopo River is one other large river basin in the SADC region which extends across Botswana, South Africa, Mozambique and Zimbabwe (Figure 2). The Limpopo Water Commission (LIMCOM) is responsible for managing the Limpopo River while the Zambezi Water Commission (ZAMCOM) was signed by riparian states with a view to govern the use and management of the Zambezi River basin.

Managing the Zambezi River Basin has posed some planning implications on residents on either side of the river. In Zimbabwe, there are strict laws which regulate fishing activities in the river. The Environmental Management Agent requires one to have a fishing permit so as to enable them to legally fish in the Zambezi River. This is not the case in Zambia and Mozambique where citizens do not need to be holders of fishing permits so as to fish in the Zambezi River (Dhliwayo, 2009). The implication is that there is more fish on the Zimbabwean side which then compels Zambian and Mozambique fishermen to come on the Zimbabwean side of the border and harvest the seemingly abundant fish. This scenario shows how there is a lack of harmony and coordination between the regulative policies on each side of the border a situation which complicates the sustainable utilisation of the water resources and fisheries in the Zambezi River.

The other issue which concerns the Zambezi River Basin is the management of dams along the river course. Three dams (Kariba, Mulungushi and Cabora Bassa) are located along the Zambezi and Luangwa rivers and their management during different times of the year has proved to be a challenge that requires some effective management plans which harmonise development and human well-being in the different countries. When excess water accumulates in the dams during the rainy season, the flood gates are opened and this negatively affects the Mague and Zumbu communities which are downstream (Dhliwayo, 2009). As a result, there are incidences of flooding, property destruction, loss of human lives, livestock and crops. The situation is no better during the dry seasons and droughts where water is retained and stored the Kariba and Mulungushi dams, leaving the downstream communities exposed to water scarcity. Resolving such problems requires mechanisms which support co-existence among the users of the water which will ultimately contribute towards the sustainability of the water resources in the region.

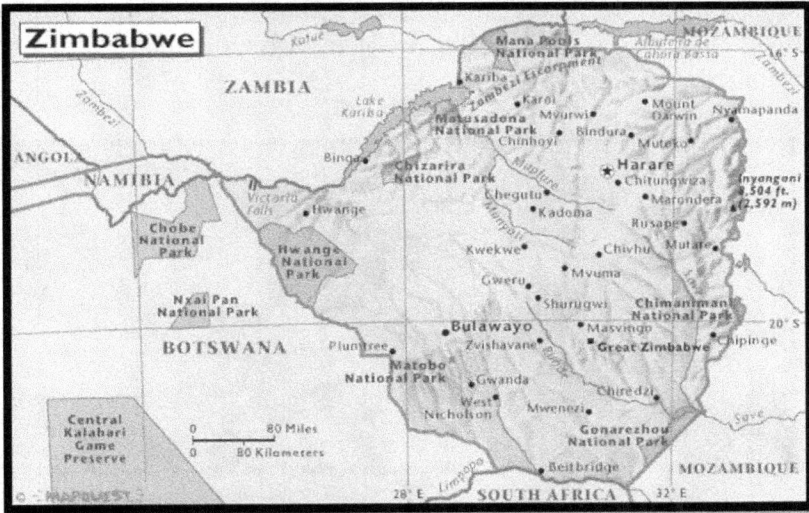

Figure 2: Map showing the River Basins bordering Zimbabwe and her neighbours

In addition to the management of water resources, issues in wildlife management are of great concern along the country's borders. This is so because there are various wildlife sanctuaries which are found along the country's borders. Gonarezhou National Park is located on the southern part of the country along the Mozambique-Zimbabwe border; Mana Pools National Park is located on the northern part of the Zimbabwe along the Zimbabwe-Zambia border, while Hwange National Park is along the Zimbabwe-Botswana border (Figure 2). Wildlife is associated with opportunities and constraints on communities and these have to be managed and planned for in an amicable way so that there is conservation of the wild life which is done in ways that benefit communities on either side of the borders.

Opportunities of wildlife along the Zimbabwe's borders include promotion of tourism which is usually integrated and supported by the CAMPFIRE programme. Eco-tourism in relation to some landmarks such as Victoria Falls which is shared between Zimbabwe and Zambia is also important (Figure 3). However, there are always inherent challenges associated with wildlife, for example, attacks on humans and livestock, damage on crops and infrastructure such as housing and spread of diseases such as anthrax and foot and mouth from some wild animals to domestic animals. In this regard, there is a need to ensure that wildlife is managed such that there are few problems which emerge as mentioned in this paragraph.

Figure 3: Victoria Falls one of the Seven Wonders of the World shared between Zimbabwe and Zambia

In managing wildlife and communities at the edge, the establishment of trans-border conservation areas has been hailed by many proponents. These trans-border conservation areas make it possible for the wildlife to roam freely without taking note of the restrictive artificial boundaries. Muqayi and Manyeruke (2015) demonstrate the challenges of wildlife roaming around the Chirundu border and at times attacking travellers. The human-wildlife conflicts along the Gonarezhou National Park where elephants damage people's crops come with diverse interpretations on the Zimbabwean as well as the Mozambique side (Figure 4). The CAMPFIRE project on the Zimbabwean side mean that citizens benefit while their counterparts on the Mozambique side suffer the brunt of crop damage. The Greater Limpopo Trans-frontier Conservation Area which constitutes the Chiredzi district on the Zimbabwe side is a critical area.

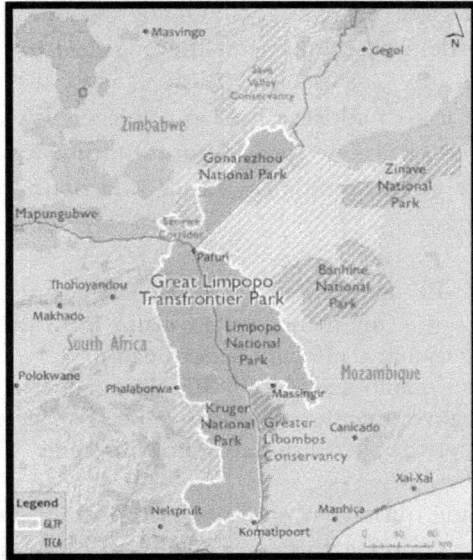

Figure 4: The Greater Limpopo Trans Frontier Conservation Area which straddles across the borders of Zimbabwe, Mozambique and South Africa
Source: Peace Parks (2017)

From 2013, the outbreak of the civil war in Mozambique has greatly compromised security issues along the 1 000 km Zimbabwe-Mozambique border (Jakwa, 2017). The civil war has spilled into Zimbabwe where the communities living along the border in Manicaland province is increasingly complaining of cattle rustling, abductions and killing of civilians. It has been alleged these crimes are mainly conducted by the Renamo and Mozambican soldiers who are armed and have the motive rustle cattle from the province so as to feed their army (Chiketo, 2017). In addition to the rustling of cattle, the fighters and soldiers have been reported to loot houses along the border as well as victimising civilians. The result has been retaliation from some villagers who end up raiding cattle pens in Mozambique for revenge (Jakwa, 2017). Matimaire (2016) reports that unemployed youths in Nyanga and Burma Valley were being lured by Renamo rebel soldiers to join their army. Such a situation poses security threats as these youths end up becoming a threat to society. Subsequently, some residents have resorted to moving around with machetes which make the region very unsafe especially for women and children who are easy targets. Droughts and high proportion of refuges in the borderland exacerbates the plight of the citizens residing in the region.

However, efforts to address the on-going civil war and unrest along the Zimbabwe-Mozambique border are compromised by the selfish stances which the governments on either side of the border take. Jakwa (2017) argues that:

> ...both ZANU-PF and Frelimo have been reluctant to move beyond liberation rhetoric – the mandate they claim from their independence legacy – undermining effective coordination of responses to the challenge. The Frelimo and ZANU-PF alliance hangs on tenterhooks, with neither government willing to appear weak in the face of increasing domestic political and economic instability

From the foregoing quotation, it emerges that the issue of security along national borders requires efforts from both sides. Mutual agreement and shared interest have to be at stake such that governments prioritise human safety and livelihoods rather than pursue their selfish agenda at the expense of human well-being.

Unlike EVD and river blindness diseases which plague West Africa, cholera and typhoid are prominent in sub-Saharan African countries. It is argued by World Health Organisation (2009: 2) that the outbreak of cholera has taken on a sub-regional dimension with cases being reported from neighbouring countries in South Africa, Mozambique, Malawi, Zambia and Botswana. In 2008 the cholera outbreak in Zimbabwe spread to the South Africa side where cases were reported in Limpopo and Mpumalanga, which eventually prompted the South African government to provide assistance on the Zimbabwean side of the border. The outbreak of cholera in Zambia in December 2017 affected 3 000 Zambians and claimed 70 lives while 155 cases were reported in Mozambique (Thompson, 2018). The main reason for the spread of cholera in the region is attributed to the porous borders which allow citizens to move freely between the countries in the region (NewsDay, 09 January, 2018. This is the same with West Africa where the EDV spread rapidly in 2014 owing to porous borders. In response to this outbreak, the Zimbabwean government has been on high alert where it has tightened its borders through screening travellers with a view to detect and restrict entry of infected persons into the country (Mashaya, 2018).

Health issues along borders also include diseases among livestock and wildlife. Diseases such as foot and mouth usually attack cattle, yet most of the cattle in Zimbabwe are reared in Matabeleland. This province is in close proximity to the Zimbabwe-Botswana border. On the other hand, the economy of Botswana is also supported by cattle production considering their arid conditions which do not favour crop production. The economic and political upheavals that characterised Zimbabwe during the early 2000s resulted in most Zimbabweans crossing the border into Botswana in search of greener pastures. Coupled with the outbreak of foot and mouth in Zimbabwe, in 2003 the Botswana government erected a 500km fence along the Zimbabwean border with the view to keep out infected cattle from the Zimbabwean border (Carrol, 2003). However, some proponents argue that the fence was erected to restrict illegal flow of Zimbabweans into Botswana owing to the economic crisis in the country at the time.

Conclusion and Recommendations

The chapter concludes that spatial and physical considerations and border management in Zimbabwe is an area that requires committed effort and attention from the government if sustainability is to be achieved as espoused in the different conventions and protocols which guide and regulate sustained socio-economic development of various sectors in the country. Unlike the other regions which are located in the country, it emerges that borderlands in the country are synonymous with a plethora of socio-economic and environmental challenges which are frequently exacerbates by the geo-political and economic crisis which have characterised the country since the early 2000s. It emerges that borderlands in Zimbabwe as somehow marginalised and given little priority with regards the spatial and physical planning. This is evident from the gross deficit of infrastructure and basic services which characterise border towns such as Chirundu, Beitbridge and Nyamapanda. The other issue concerns the predicament which is faced by those citizens who live on the borders and are vulnerable to wildlife which damage their crops as well as posing a threat on human life.

Chapter Four | Chirisa & Rajab Matamanda

75

Security issues along the Zimbabwe-Mozambique border are a threat and infringement of human rights espoused in the Constitution of Zimbabwe Amendment (No. 20). In as much as wildlife is associated with much benefits there tend to be benefits which accrue on one side of the border owing to disparities in development, an example is the case of the Greater Limpopo Trans-frontier Conservation area where tourists are more on the South African side owing to a developed infrastructure on that side. Dividends from natural resources do not really benefit communities leaving with the dangers.

In relation to the foregoing discussion the chapter recommends the following:

- Recognise that borders are not rigid lines which can be draw; rather they have to be flexible and consider the socio-cultural and environmental factors.
- Harmonise land use regulations and management systems that regulate shared natural resources so that they are developed on mutual agreement and cooperation among heads of states and the communities living on the edges.
- Promote regional integration which is premised on citizen participation so that the concerns of communities on either side of the border are factored in the development of socio-economic and environmental issues impacting on land use along the borders.
- Formulate effective and functional river basin management plans which take into consideration the needs of upstream and downstream communities so that there is limited conflicts which may ensure as a result of utilisation of water and fishing activities in the river courses.
- Invest in trans-frontier natural resources management schemes which help to reduce conflicts along the borders especially with regards use of natural resources.

References

Attree, L., Dodd, H., Smith, S., Stepanova, E., Pitts-Kiefer, S. 2014. Measuring and understanding the Impact of terrorism: Global Terrorism Index. New York: Institute for Economics and Peace.

Bentsi-Enchill, K. 1976. The Traditional Legal System of Africa. In *Property and Trust, vol.6, International Encyclopaedia of Comparative Law.* Pp. 2-138

Carrillo G, Uribe F, Lucio R, Ramirez Lopez A, Korc M. The United States–Mexico border environmental public health: the challenges of working with two systems. *Pan American Journal of Public Health*, 47: 1-7.

Carroll, R. 2003. Botswana Erects 300-Mile Electrified Fence to Keep Cattle (and Zimbabweans) Out. The Guardian (10 September 2003).

CDC (2016). CDC's Response to the 2014-2016 Ebola Epidemic-West Africa and United States. *MMWR Supplement* 65(3): 1-106

Chiketo, B. 2017. Zim-Moza Border Conflict Escalates. DailyNews Online]. Available at: https://www.dailynews.co.zw/articles/2017/0 2/12/zim-moza-border-conflict-escalates. Accessed on 27 March, 2018.

Cook, N and Salaam-Blyther, T. 2014. *Ebola: 2014 Outbreak in West Africa*. Available Online: https://fas.org/sgp/crs/row/IF00044.pdf. Accessed 20 March, 2018.

Dhliwayo, M. 2009. Legal Aspects of Trans-Boundary Natural Resources Management in Southern Africa. Paper Prepared for the IASCP Conference.

European Commission. 2014. *Borders and Security*. Brussels: European Commission.

Fischhendler, I., Dinar, S and Katz, D. 2011. The Politics of Unilateral Environmentalism: Cooperation and Con°ict over Water Management along the Israeli-Palestinian Border. Global Environmental Politics, 11(1): 36-61.

Foltz, W. J. 1981. Modernization and Nation-Building: The Social Mobilization Model Reconsidered. In Merrit, R. L and Russett, B. M (ed.) *From National Development to Global Community*. London: George Allen and Unwin.

Gustavan, K., Sodahlon, Y and Bosh, S. 2016. Cross-border collaboration for neglected tropical disease efforts—Lessons learned from onchocerciasis control and elimination in the Mano River Union (West Africa). *Globalisation and Health*, 12(44): 1-5

Hensel, P. 1999. Charting a Course to Conflict: Territorial Issues and Interstate Conflict. In Diehl, P, The Road Map to War. Nashvile, Vanderbilt University Press.

Herbst, J. 2000. States and Power in Africa: Comparative Lessons in Authority and Control. Princeton: Princeton University Press.

Homedes, N and Ugalde, A. 2003. Globalization and Health at the United States-Mexico Border. *Public Health Matters*, 93(12): 2016-2022.

Huang, Y (2010). *Comparing the H1N1 Crises and Responses in the US and China.* NTS Working Paper Series No.1, Singapore: RSIS Centre for Non-Traditional Security (NTS) Studies.

Jackson, R. H and Rosberg, C. G. 1985. The Marginality of African States. In Carter and O'Meara (ed.) *African Independence: The First Twenty-Five Years.* Bloomington: Indiana University Press.

Jakwa, T. 2017. The Zimbabwe-Mozambique Border Conflict. Foreign Brief. Available at: https://www.foreignbrief.com/africa/zimbabwe-mozambique-border-conflict/. Accessed on 27 March, 2018.

Jing, A. 2015. *A History of the Great Wall of China.* (Translated by Wang, G and Wang, A. Y.). Hong Kong: SCPG Publishing Corporation.

Maganda, C. 2012. Border Water Culture in Theory and Practice: Political Behaviour on the Mexico-U.S. Border. *Journal of Political Ecology*, 19: 81-93

Mancini, F. 2013. Uncertain Borders: Territorial Disputes in Asia. *Analysis*, 180: 1-9.

Matimaire, K. 2016. Zimbabwe Borders under Threat. Financial Gazette [Online]. Available at: http://www.financialgazette.co.zw/zimbabwe-borders-under-threat/. Accessed on 27 March, 2018.

Mashaya, B. 2018. *Govt Screening Cholera at Borders.* DailyNews. Available at: https://www.dailynews.co.zw/articles/2018/01/30/govt-screening-cholera-at-borders. Accessed 25 March, 2018

NewsDay. 2018 . Government says Prepared to deal with Cholera outbreak from Zambia, all borders on alert. Available at: http://www.newzimbabwe.com/news-41030-Zim+on+Cholera+alert+as+61+die+in+Zambia/news.aspx. Accessed 25 March, 2018

Nkiwane, S. M. 1993. Border Issues and Conflicts in Southern Africa. *Border Issues and Conflicts in Southern Africa*, 25(1): 67-76

Nyoni, M. 2018. *Crime rate spikes in Beitbridge.* NewsDay. Online URL: https://www.newsday.co.zw/2018/03/crime-rate-spikes-in-beitbridge/. Accessed 26 March, 2018.

OECD. 2011. Improving Service Delivery and Reducing Clearing Times at Chirundu Border Post. Pretoria: OECD.

Rodríguez-Saldaña, J. 2005. Challenges and opportunities in border health. Prev Chronic Dis. Online URL: http://www.cdc.gov/pcd/iss ues/2005/jan/ 04_0099.htm.

SADC. 2015. *SADC @ 35 Success Stories*. Cape Town: SADC.

Thompson, J. 2018. *Zimbabwe Gets Tough at borders to try to contain cholera outbreak*. BusinessDay. Online URL: https://www.businesslive.co.za/ bd/world/africa/2018-02-02-zimbabwe-gets-tough-at-borders-to-try-to-contain-cholera-outbreak/. Accessed 25 March, 2018.

Trouwborst, A., Fleurke, F and Dubrulle, J. 2016. Border Fences and their Impacts on Large Carnivores, Large Herbivores and Biodiversit y: An International Wildlife Law Perspective. *RIGEL*, 25(3): 291-306

United Nations. 2016. *The Sustainable Development Goals Report: 2016*. Washington, D.C: United Nations.

Weber, A. 2012. *Boundaries with Issues: Soft Border Management as a Solution?* Berlin: Friedrich-Ebert-Stiftung, Africa Department.

Wiegand, K. 2011. Enduring Territorial Disputes: Strategies of Bargaining, Coercive Diplomacy, and Settlement. Athens: University of Georgia Press.

World Health Organisation. 2009. *Cholera Country Profile: Zimbabwe*. Harare: World Health Organisation.

CHAPTER FIVE

The Impact of the Automated System for Customs Data (ASYCUDA) in Promoting Trade Facilitation at Zimbabwe's Borders.

Solomon Muqayi

Introduction

Border management is a global cause for concern due to its impact on the country's development. The complex issues surrounding border management have motivated many researchers, strategists and planners to explore measures to combat all factors constraining the effective management of border posts. This chapter looks at the effectiveness of the Automated System for Customs Data (ASYCUDA) which was adopted by the Zimbabwe Revenue Authority (ZIMRA), Customs Division, at Zimbabwe border posts, with specific reference to the following issues: border management, custom clearance systems and gaps in the ZIMRA's anti-corruption initiatives. The chapter also examines the role played by COMESA in supporting the ASYCUDA clearing system in Zimbabwe thereby raising the importance of regionalism in customs clearance. The Zimbabwe Revenue Authority (ZIMRA) uses the ASYCUDA for clearing commercial consignments at the ports of entry (border posts and airports). It is a web-based system. Traders are required to be registered at the ZIMRA offices in order for them to access the ASYCUDA system. An Automation system is defined as a service that supports the implementation of contemporary customs management practices. The customs automation system is one of the most fundamental tools used in order to improve customs efficiency and effectiveness (OECD, 2005). The main aim of installing customs automation systems at ports of entry (air ports and border posts) is to serve both the private and public interests. Thus, the ASYCUDA actually helps to reduce both administrative and trading costs to both customs authorities and business dealers thereby improving the way of managing borders.

The ASYCUDA was developed and is being maintained by the United Nations Conference on Trade and Development (UNCTAD). It is a computerised customs management system which covers trade procedures. The system handles customs declarations, suspense procedures, transit and accounting procedures (ASYCUDA Organisation, 2014). It takes into consideration the international standards and codes developed by the International Organisation for Standardisation (IOS), World Customs Organisation (WCO) and the United Nations. It can be configured to meet or suit the characteristics of an individual nation's customs regions, legislation and national tariffs. During the period covered by this study, ASYCUDA was being utilised in 80 developing countries as of 2017 (ASYCUDA Organisation, 2017). In order to have a successful installation, the ASYCUDA requires careful planning of many activities such as training of technicians and customs officials.

Conceptual Framework

Trade facilitation

Trade facilitation is a broad concept with no single standard definition ESCAP (2002), Hellqvist, (2002:6), OECD, (2000:5); Taneja (2004:8), UN, (2002:1); Wilson, Mann and Otsuki, (2003:369). The use of the term 'trade facilitation' varies in the literature since each definition serves the particular attention or purpose of each organisation. Trade facilitation can be defined either in simple terms, or in the narrow sense or in the broad sense, and it can be identified at different levels depending on scope and areas. In simple terms, trade facilitation is often defined as the simplification and standardisation of international trade procedures and other administrative procedures related to the transportation of goods (Hellqvist, 2002:6; OECD, 2002:5; Taxation and Customs Union, 2007; UN, 2002:1). In the narrow sense, trade facilitation refers to the improvement of procedural efficiency associated with the movement of goods across national borders (ICC, 2003; Wilson et al., 2003). A broader definition of trade facilitation focuses on the improvement of the 'environment' where trade transactions take place. This includes the removal of non-tariff barriers, the improvement of infrastructure and facilities, the transparency of regulatory environments and the harmonisation of standards and related laws and regulations (OECD, 2005:2; UNECE, 2002; Wilson et al., 2003:369; World Bank, 2005:9).

In some studies, the term 'trade facilitation' is used to cover a wide range of areas such as government regulations and controls, business efficiency, transportation and shipping, information and communication technologies, health and safety standards, and financial requirements (Taneja, 2004:3; UNECE, 2002:3). However, the preferred definition in some studies is a wide-ranging one but does not cover the physical infrastructure, non-tariff barriers (NTBs), tariff negotiations or trade promotion (Staples, 1998:2; UN, 2002:1).

Much of the literature uses the definition adopted by the World Trade Organisation (WTO) in which trade facilitation refers to "the simplification and harmonisation of international trade procedures, where trade procedures are the activities, practices and formalities involved in collecting, presenting, communicating and processing the data required for the movement of goods in international trade" (Hellqvist 2002:6; OECD, 2002:6; OECD 2005:2; SITPRO, 2005; Taneja, 2004:8). While the definition and the scope of the term trade facilitation vary in the studies, there is a general consensus that trade facilitation refers to the simplification, harmonisation and standardisation of international trade procedures. This understanding of the concept and the definition of it are widely used in the studies of the international organisations such as the WTO and the Organisation for Economic Cooperation and Development (OECD), among other international organisations. Some trade facilitation studies use a narrow definition, which focuses for the most part on the improvement of trade procedures. Other studies, however, broaden the concept of trade facilitation and its definition to embrace the trade environment. In general, trade facilitation covers areas such as transportation, the regulatory requirements, and business efficiency and information technologies. However, studies which focus on the improvement of the trade environment encompass areas such as infrastructure and facilities, tariff and non-tariff barriers, transparency and trade promotion while other studies exclude these issues from both the definition and the scope of trade facilitation.

This study uses the widely accepted definition adopted by the WTO since it is an international organisation which sets global rules and standards for trade between nations, and is thus considered the core of a multilateral trading system in which trade rules are set on a consensus basis and applied equally to all member countries with a balance of rights and obligations. In particular, the WTO is the predominant organisation concerned with trade facilitation negotiations and international trade procedures (Chibwesha, 2010:34). In addition, customs administration is a central government agency involved in activities related to the movement of goods across international borders. Thus, trade facilitation basically refers to the simplification, standardisation and harmonisation of customs procedures. In addition to adopting the meaning of trade facilitation provided by the WTO, the study also considers trade facilitation in the customs context provided by the World Customs Organization (WCO). In this context, trade facilitation means "the simplification and harmonisation of international trade procedures" (WCO, 2007:11) with avoidance of unnecessary trade restrictiveness while at the same time enhancing the efficiency and effectiveness of customs controls in accordance with international standards (WCO, 2008:4).

This review of the literature also examined the impact of trade facilitation on customs and administrative procedures as well as the specific issues of technical regulations and automated systems. Further, the review examined the international framework, strategy papers and recommended practices that relate to trade facilitation and customs operations. The literature identified the core components of trade facilitation, which generally include the improvement of trade and customs procedures, the enhancement of cooperation among concerned authorities and trading communities, the improvement of customs controls and enforcement, and the implementation of information and communication technology.

Impact of Trade Facilitation on Customs Systems and Procedures

Recent research at the OECD (2005b, 2007:36) examined the trade effects and impacts of customs and administrative procedures on trade facilitation. The OECD (2005b) studied the economic impact of trade facilitation in general and the specific issues of customs systems and procedures in particular. The data analysis of this study is based on empirical data derived from "country experiences and recent quantitative estimates of the economic impact of improvements in border procedures" (OECD, 2005b:6). The 2007 OECD study provides quantitative evidence of the effects of non-tariff measures on trade flows.

These two studies by the OECD (2005b, 2007) presented evidence that customs and administrative procedures have substantial effects on trade flows. Inefficient customs systems and procedures resulted in "delayed and unreliable delivery, costly customs clearance and missed business opportunities" (OECD, 2005b:26). At the same time, the simplification and harmonisation of customs procedures had a significant positive impact on trade facilitation, trade flows and investment (OECD, 2007:18; Walsh, 2006). The results further showed that all countries could benefit from the efficiency and effectiveness of customs and administrative procedures. Importantly, the OECD (2005b, 2007) reached the same conclusion as the studies of Taneja (2004) and UNECE (2003a) that trade facilitation measures are particularly significant for developing countries, and the greatest benefits of trade facilitation to these countries come mainly from improvements in port and customs efficiency.

Technical Regulations and Automation

Messerlin and Zarrouk (2000) and the OECD (2005c) provide two major research studies related to the specific issues of customs procedures, technical regulations and automated systems within the area of trade facilitation. One of the studies done by OECD in 2005 focused on quantitative estimates of the importance of trade facilitation, multilateral responses to trade facilitation and the enforcement of both technical and customs regulations. The OECD research also addressed trade facilitation issues in general and examined technical regulations and customs procedures in particular. It found that there are some trade conflicts between developed and developing countries regarding trade regulations and customs procedures (OECD, 2005c). Developed countries criticised the restrictions in the trade regulations of developing countries while developing countries complained about the 'spaghetti bowl' of rules of origin included in the customs procedures of the developed countries (Messerlin and Zarrouk, 2000:578). The study suggested that trade conflicts between developed and developing countries can be solved by establishing clear essential requirements for bilateral or regional agreements. Also, the enforcement of trade regulations and customs procedures should be discussed in the global framework. The study also highlighted the need for cooperation between the WTO and the World Customs Organisation (WCO) on the implementation of the revised Kyoto Convention on customs best practices.

In a review of studies in this field (ESCAP, 2004; UNECE, 2001; WCO, 2005a), it is notable that customs automation is considered a potential means to reduce trade transaction costs and facilitate trade while safeguarding national and social security. The WCO revised Kyoto Convention also places emphasis on the use of automation in customs systems and procedures. However, the recent study of the OECD (2005c:4) pointed out that although automation is not a 'panacea' for trade facilitation, commitment and financial sustainability are prerequisites for successful modernisation involving automation. The study further explained that automation is useful only if it serves as a tool to support the implementation of modern customs management and practices (OECD, 2005c:7). This conclusion is supported by the evidence provided by the experience of other countries that trade facilitation measures can be achieved without automation (OECD, 2005c:7).

The major concept applied for this study is the trade facilitation concept. Trade facilitation is a concept that entails the harmonisation and simplification of international trade procedures and it involves the formalities and active practices involved in presenting, collecting, communication and processing data required for the movement of goods and services in global trade (United Nations 2011). According to the World Bank (2014:01) the key tenets of trade facilitation include the simplification, standardisation and harmonisation of trade procedures. It is widely believed that trade facilitation measures increase the flow of the goods and services across the borders (Silva 2013). This study discovered that COMESA has introduced the OSBP programme in order to increase the flow of goods across the region. The application of modern border management and trade facilitation measures has been an event/activity formulated by developed countries. Polner (2014) and Doyle et al. (2011) put much attention of presenting the border management reforms implemented by the European countries. This study desisted from discussing border management from the developed countries perspective and it therefore focused on border management reforms and programmes implemented by the Zimbabwean government in order to improve trade facilitation. This study discovered that the implementation of trade facilitation at the Zimbabwe entry ports has helped a lot in addressing border protectionist challenges such as border delays, long queues, corruption and unnecessary inspections and searches at the Zimbabwean borders. The implementation of trade facilitation measures usually helps to increase a country's ability to use the benefits of market access (United Nations 2011a). COMESA has improved market access to its member states through the implementation of the Chirundu OSBP which has led to the improved flow of goods and people transiting the border. However, the main reasons for the unwillingness of developing countries to adopt trade facilitation is the understandable fear of going through the costs associated such as infrastructural requirements, operational procedures and human resources (Buyonge and Kireeva 2008:43). Thus, the implementation of trade facilitation measures poses multiple demands on limited resources of developing countries. In addition, another challenge associated with trade facilitation is that governments will have to fund the projects, programmes or reforms before seeing the benefits in relation to increased trade and revenue (OECD 2014:05). The major costs associated with implementing trade facilitation reforms include institutional costs, regulatory costs, training and education costs, equipment and infrastructure costs (World Bank 2014a). This is in line with the study findings which showed that there was only one OSBP in Zimbabwe because the country was failing to establish other OSBPs due to the huge costs associated even though the government had already approved the establishment of many OSBPs at the Zimbabwean borders.

Research Methodology

This section discusses the methodology applied to address the study objectives and research questions. The major issues outlined in this methodology include: research design, sampling and population, data gathering and data analysis. Data gathering methods used in this methodology included: interviews, observations and documentary search. These methodologies ensure the covering of both primary and secondary sources. Rahman and Yeasmin (2012:155) notes that combining primary and secondary data collection methods to overcome the intrinsic biases, weaknesses and problems that come from a single method. Thus, primary and secondary collection methods complement each other in order to improve reliability and validity of data obtained from the data collection process. The researcher conducted 17 face to face interviews with respondents from various organisations such as Zimtrade, COMES A Secretariat, Shipping and Forwarding Association of Zimbabwe (SIFA Z), Shalom Clearance Agency, Ministry of Regional Integration and Inter national Cooperation, cross border traders, Ministry of Agriculture, Mini stry of Industry and Commerce and Zimbabwe Revenue Authority (ZIM RA). The researcher applied documentary search to solicit data. In the discipline of social sciences, documentary search is a method that involves the use of wide range of documents such as books, journals, government publications, newspapers, magazines, letters, diaries, persona l notes, biographies, essays, government pronouncements and proceedin gs, internet and policy documents (Punch 2008:190). The documents collected from various institutions were helpful in providing statistics as well as a historical background of the development of Zimbabwe's border management and trade policies. The study also applied observation method to collect primary data. The researcher started conducting observations at Chirundu and Beitbridge border post in 2012. The researcher has been observing a variety of issues such as finding out how border officials interact with transiting people, the rate of border clearance, corruption and infrastructural developments. This helped a lot in identifying the challenges and benefits associated with the Automated System for Customs Data. The researcher applied content analysis to analyse data. Thus, the sub-themes designed for this study were related to various issues such as the challenges, benefits, and strategies to improve border management in Zimbabwean borders.

Discussion of Findings

The study observed that there are a wide range of factors that influence Zimbabwe to implement the ASYCUDA and these include: (1) limited human resources; (2) time factor: coping with global changes and technology; (3) rapidly growing trade flows; (4) health standards at borders; (5) environmental benefits; (6) the need to improve transparency and accountability; and (7) the increased rate of smuggling and other unscrupulous activities at the ports of entry. In Zimbabwe, the ASYCUDA is accessed by the ZIMRA officials as well as the agencies representing the importers and exporters of commercial products. The registered companies and individual entrepreneurs are given identification numbers which are used for logging on to the system. The identification number ensures that the registered traders and dealers can access Zimbabwe's ASYCUDA system from any place in the world. The traders are required to fill the Bill of Entry form before the consignment gets to a port of entry. The dealers also upload all the necessary documents such as invoices, exportation or importation permits, licences, certificates of origin, freight and insurance invoices. ZIMRA considers all the costs incurred by the consignments and uses such information for customs valuation when calculating the import duties for consignments. The major costs required by ZIMRA include all the costs and charges such as the buying price, transport costs, insurance costs and port charges among other related business costs.

The application of customs automation as well as the use of Information and Communication Technology (ICT) in facilitating trade procedures has drawn crucial attention in the COMESA meetings and workshops. Thus, the COMESA regional organisation plays a pivotal role in promoting the smooth running of the ASYCUDA for its Member States so as to improve the liberalisation of the customs procedures. According to ZIMRA (2013) "the ASYCUDA system has been adopted as the official customs computer system in the COMESA region and is being used by 19 Member States." COMESA has played a pivotal role in advising its Member States to install the latest version of ASYCUDA in their customs clearing systems. This study observed that Zambia was using an outdated version of the ASYCUDA and this was raising some challenges at Chirundu OSBP since Zimbabwe was using a latest version of referred to as ASYCUDA World. The use of different versions of the ASYCUDA at Chirundu OSBP by both Zimbabwe and Zambia was raising a plethora of challenges resulting in the slow operation of the customs clearance at the OSBP. COMESA played a fundamental role in convincing Zambia to upgrade its system from ASYCUDA 2.7 to ASYCUDA World. This Study also noted that COMESA negotiates with UNCTAD on behalf of its members. The major aspects negotiated between COMESA and UNCTAD include the prices of software updates, rules and regulations, operating procedures and procures for conducting training and education procedures. Furthermore, COMESA provides some funding to its Member States so as to provide training facilities to the customs officials. Indications are that COMESA plays an active role in improving the operations of the ASYCUDA to its Member States. This actually helps to improve the liberalisation of customs procedures within the COMESA region thereby facilitating the reduction of trade barriers such as border delays and long queues at the borders.

This study observed that the efforts carried out by the Zimbabwean government in updating the ASYCUDA versions towards the attainment of trade liberalisation were very positive. The implementation of automation systems at the borders helps to reduce border delays and other related barriers to trade at the borders thereby enhancing the free flow of goods and services. The OECD (2005:7) indicates that "Smooth trade flows are paramount in many countries that are dependent on the just- in -time delivery and global supply chain systems. Predictable border services, customs clearance time and trade transaction costs are important factors when companies consider investing or doing business in a country." Thus, automation helps to reduce the time spent at the border posts. However, automation alone is not a solution for maximising the benefits of trade facilitation and trade liberalisation. Thus, customs automation systems should be complemented by the reduction of tariff levels as well as the removal of quotas and subsidies. This may eventually improve efforts to reduce trade protectionism at the same time enhancing the importance of liberalism.

This study found that the successful implementation of customs automation systems is dependent upon such factors as the availability of related technologies, consistent electricity supply, human and financial resources, training programmes, the availability of local maintenance systems, reliable computer hardware suppliers, consistent supply of software updates, infrastructure and reliable internet and other network facilities. However, failure to properly meet the above-mentioned factors usually results in the slow operation of ASYCUDA thereby leading to slow clearances at the ports of entry. The slow pace of clearance at the ports of entry usually led to long queues and high costs of doing business on the part of traders. Governments should, therefore, ensure the smooth operation of the ASYCUDA so as to avoid unnecessary trade barriers at the ports of entry.

This study noted that the ASYCUDA is being used by both developing and developed countries. According to the ASYCUDA Organisation (2014) "84 countries are using ASYCUDA at the present moment (United Nations, 2011)." Zimbabwe started using ASYCUDA customs clearing software in 1991. In 2001, Zimbabwe migrated to the use of a better version of ASYCUDA which is referred to as ASYCUDA (Zhou, 2016). It was the first country to start using ASYCUDA throughout the COMESA regional bloc. Zimbabwe was also the first country in the COMESA to utilise ASYCUDA World. It started migrating to ASYCUDA World in September 2011 (ZIMRA 2014). ASYCUDA World has diversified functions such as incorporating a customs broker module and risk management module where customers can register declaration from any place in the world. Thus, clients can register their consignments at their offices, homes, or any other place outside Zimbabwe (OECD (2005). With this version of the ASYCUDA, there is no need to register declarations at ZIMRA offices as the traders can launch their declarations on the internet. Furthermore, the customer broker module can also allow customers to monitor payments made for their importations. Significantly, ZIMRA was also the first revenue authority in the COMESA region to migrate to ASYCUDA World and this has attracted lot of interest from other states. Primarily, ZIMRA installed ASYCUDA World to 11 stations that include: Harare International Airport, Mutare, Masvingo, Gweru, Bulawayo port, and Harare port, Forbes, Victoria Falls, Plumtree and Beitbridge. It later on spread the installation process thereby covering other stations such as the Chirundu OSBP, Nyamapanda, Kariba and Kazungula as well as five inland stations such ss Hwange, Zvishavane, Chiredzi, Kadoma and Kwekwe (ZIMRA, 2013). These actions suggest that Zimbabwe is responsive in terms of matching the changes that occur within the realm of global automation.

This study found that, the successful implementation of the ASYCUDA also relies on long term political commitment. The government has to maintain positive relations with the suppliers of the ASYCUDA software. In addition, the administration of customs procedures and regulations requires a good relationship between policy makers (Ministry of Finance) and those mandated to implement (Silva, 2013). In the case of Zimbabwe, it was noted that there is a smooth relationship between the Ministry of Finance and the ZIMRA Department with regard to the operations of the ASYCUDA. Furthermore, the system requires to be updated on a regular basis, and the government should be willing to release money to purchase modern software and hardware on a regular basis. During the period covered by the study, the GoZ was fully supporting purchase of ASYCUDA software updates and Zimbabwe was always the first COMESA member state to utilise the latest versions of ASYCUDA. However, poor political relations between government and technicians may obstruct the effectiveness and efficiency of the ASYCUDA. Thus, in the case of Zimbabwe, ZIMRA technicians were not given favourable salaries and this was causing a serious brain drain. These ASYCUDA technicians were leaving Zimbabwe in order to look for greener pastures. The study, therefore suggests that the GoZ should increase the salaries of the ASYCUDA technicians so as to reduce unnecessary brain drain.

Benefits of the ASYCUDA

The researcher noted that the application of the ASYCUDA in the Zimbabwean customs system is associated with a wide range of benefits and advantages. This study, therefore, designed categories indicating the benefits of the ASYCUDA. The three major categories designed by the study are: (1) trade related benefits; (2) administrative benefits; and (3) law enforcement.

a. Trade related benefits

(1)The use of the ASYCUDA makes it easier to collect trade statistics. The application of the ASYCUDA makes it easier to calculate the quantity of inputs and exports cleared per day or per year; (2) trade transactions can be conducted without using any paper work; (3) biometrics are used to improve the security status for logging in (Chibwesha, 2010:34). The application of the ASYCUDA ensures safety on the part of traders; and (4) the implementation of the customs automation system has helped to lower trade transaction costs at ports of entry. Thus, it ensures that traders launch their consignments before getting to the borders and do not spend too much time at the borders (Nkwemu, 2011). Thus, the ASYCUDA helps to the reduce time spent by traders at the borders. One can therefore argue that the ASYCUDA system helps to address border protectionism as it helps to reduce the amount of time spent at the borders; (5) ASYCUDA World enhances the exercise of trade facilitation and trade expansion since it is designed to suit international standards and codes such as WCO, Free and Secure Trade (FAST), UN, ISO and WTO. Thus, it enhances increased services for the trade community through easy internet access, standardisation, normalisation, simpler procedures and documentation; (6) the registration of countries is conducted regardless of geographical boundaries; (7) the application of the ASYCUDA helps to reduce errors in the customs clearance system ((Fugazza, 2010). "Chile's implementation of the EDI system brought significant benefits to the trading community. The number of data imputing errors fell from 14% to 2%" (OECD, 2005:14/World Bank, 2013). Unnecessary errors may escalate costs either for the traders or the government. Overvaluation of consignments directly raises some costs for the traders. Traders with the overvalued consignments will therefore incur business losses.

b. Administrative benefits

This study noted that the use of ASYCUDA in customs management systems ensures that: (1) revenue accounting and statistical capabilities are improved. The application of ASYCUDA enhances the development of post clearance audit capabilities for accounting information management and post clearance audits (COMESA, 2010). It makes it simpler and easier to aggregate data at local, regional and international levels. In addition, it improves the ability to make quicker economic decisions; (2) E-government: it is designed in a way that fully supports e-government as well as the capacity to link with the external organisational or external governmental database and systems; (3) ASYCUDA world is compatible with any type of laser printer; (4) The ASYCUDA system is difficult to connive. It is a very complicated and sensitive mechanism which is not easy to interfere with. This system reflects all users logged on at a certain time. It shows all transactions going on within the system at a particular time and this makes it easier for ZIMRA officers to identify those people trying to manipulate the system. For this reason, one can make the observation that the ASYCUDA system has tight security measures (Mubaiwa, 2013). Thus, it reduces incidents of corruption; (5) it enhances fast clearance of consignments; (6) it increases convenience for traders since they can access the system from any place in the world. As a result of this, it reduces the time spent by cross-border traders at the borders; (7) it guarantees improved valuation of consignments which may eventually help to increase government revenue; (8) it is easier to trace issues of irregularities. In the event that the consignment has already reached Harare the traders may not need to go back to the border posts. The irregularities may be addressed at any ZIMRA offices; and (9) the installation of the ASYCUDA system at Zimbabwean borders is considered a vital necessity in most customs-related issues. During the period covered by the study, the ASYCUDA was considered as the most reliable and cheapest customs clearance software available anywhere. In addition, the use of the ASYCUDA was considered as a cheaper option than for the country to develop its own software for use in the customs processes (Erasmus, 2013). According to the International Monetary Fund (2013) acquiring an existing software package such as micro clear, ASYCUDA, TIMS, TATIS or SOFI is less costly than developing original software. If a country develops its own software it means it will incur more costs related to updating and maintaining it; (10) the study found that the ASYCUDA system is more effective than paper-based customs clearing systems. A study conducted by the OECD on New Zealand shows that "over 98% of electronically lodged import entries were processed within 50 minutes (Dube and Ngoma, 2012). The New Zealand Customs Services envisages the processing of Electronic Data Interchange (EDI) import entries within 24 hours. Thus, the utilisation of the ASYCUDA improves the rate of clearing consignments at ports of entry; (11) Managers and supervisors can oversee and monitor transactions even when they are outside their normal workplaces, for example when they are on vacation or at workshops and seminars among other out of office environments. Thus, the ASYCUDA world is flexible since it allows customs officers to carry out their office work from any place in the world; (12) ASYCUDA World is designed to function in different and difficult telecommunication systems and it also operates via GSM networks that are widely available in developing countries (Cox and Warr, 2014:78). Thus, it is flexible as it can be used by African nations without facing network challenges; (13) the implementation of this automation system can lead to improved customs control and improved government functions. It can also promote a culture of cooperation and interaction between government and business (both companies and individuals). In Zimbabwe, the application of the ASYCUDA has helped to improve the relations between ZIMRA officials and traders; and (14) the ASYCUDA helps to improve security in the revenue collection system (Draper, 2012). This study found that Zimbabwe as a sovereign nation has gained a lot from the ASYCUDA system in the sense that it is now able to meet objectives related to the maintenance of human, social and national security. The security features associated with the ASYCUDA system forbid external spies from accessing important national customs data.

c. Law enforcement

The study observed that the application of ASYCUDA helps to improve the enforcement of laws. Such enforcement is enhanced through the following ways: (1) national tariff rates are loaded into the ASYCUDA system, hence, it reduces personal biases and errors on the calculations of import duties and export taxes; (2) ASYCUDA increases customs control capabilities, for example, online access to external databases, emergency control and easier assessment of the national revenue collection system (Draper, 2012). Thus, ASYCUDA enhances a full range of modern enforcement capabilities and it also improves risk assessment and security functions; and (3) it improves accountability and transparency. Thus, the proper utilisation of ASYCUDA ensures that similar tariff rates are applied in all cases regardless of political status. When tariff rates are calculated manually, customs officials can be forced to reduce import duties for the consignments owned by top government officials (COMESA, 2010). The application of ASYCUDA for customs valuations, therefore, reduces flaws in the customs valuation system. Precisely, it enhances the applicability of the rule of law doctrine in a nation.

Challenges and Costs Affecting the Effectiveness of ASYCUDA

The study noted that the major challenges affecting the operations of ASYCUDA in Zimbabwe include: (1) internet connectivity challenges. During the period covered by the study, internet connection at the borders was not consistent. This was, therefore, affecting the effectiveness of the ASYCDA clearance system since it directly depends on the internet. Traders and truck drivers with large commercial consignments were forced to wait in queues up until the internet connections were restored (COMESA, 2010). This then negatively affected the flow of goods passing through the border thereby negatively impacting on the COMESA regional agenda of improving the flow of goods and services transiting the borders; (2) power cuts: during the period covered by the study, Zimbabwe was facing severe challenges emanating from power cuts. Power cuts affect border operations in many ways such as the switching off of computers with the result that internet servers are also affected. The ASYCUDA system uses the internet so the power cuts restrict the use of the customs clearance system by ZIMRA officials; (3) Lack of knowledge: the study observed that ASYCUDA is a complex system which has to be operated by well-educated, experienced and competent staff (Draper, 2012) . During the period covered by the study, Zimbabwe was facing a severe brain drain. Experienced personnel were leaving ZIMRA for greener pastures. Those workers who were working in the ASYCUDA department of ZIMRA were in high demand in other countries. ZIMRA was, therefore, continuously recruiting new personnel to fill the gaps left by the personnel now recruited elsewhere in other countries. This was directly affecting the quality of services offered by ZIMRA, especially in the department of the ASYCUDA; (4) the lack of training programmes: the study noted that ASYCUDA system just like any other ICT programme is ever-changing and, therefore, requires its personnel to attend regular training programmes and refresher courses (COMESA, 2011). During the period covered by the study, Zimbabwe as a nation was experiencing economic hardships and ZIMRA was no longer conducting its training programmes with the usual frequency. This was, therefore, affecting the effective operation of ASYCUDA; (5) the study noted that the automated systems incur substantial operating and updating costs that must then be borne by the nation. It is reported that updating ASYCUDA software requires at least US$2 million (OECD, 2013). Customs automation systems cost US$5 million in Chile and $5 million Jamaica respectively (World Bank, 2013); and (6) during the period covered by the study, traders were expected to undergo physical registration at the ZIMRA offices in order for them to utilise the ASYCUDA (Ramesh, 2011). This added unnecessary costs to the traders. ZIMRA should, therefore, conduct an online registration process so that traders would not have to physically visit ZIMRA offices. This may help to reduce the costs of doing business.

Strategies for Improving Zimbabwe's Border Management

This study noted that Zimbabwe has embarked on several strategies in order to improve border management. These strategies have the main aim of reducing border delays and barriers affecting trade at the ports of entry and these include: (1) ZIMRA was installing a solar power system at all border posts. This solar system was connected to batteries so as to provide power during the day and the night (UNECA, 2013). This system was intended to address the challenges associated with power cuts thereby ensuring that the computers and electrical gadgets would not stop operating; (2) ZIMRA was introducing an automation of all processes, for example the issuance of temporary import or export permits. This was intended to make the clearing system easier; (3) staff development programmes: during the period covered by the study ZIMRA introduced a school that was operating at Kurima House in Harare (Shayanowako, 2013:34). This school was offering training facilities to ZIMRA officials. This was helping to improve the quality of work; (4) ZIMRA was working tirelessly in promoting constant connectivity at all the border posts and at the Chirundu border post there was a shift to internet use (Angwenyi, 2014). The shift effectively meant moving from the use of the outdated document filing system to use of the internet databases through optic fibre infrastructure installed at the Chirundu OSBP. Consequently, internet connection became consistent and more reliable. This development helped improve the rate of trade facilitation in the sense that the flow of people and goods transiting the borders was no longer affected by challenges resulting from internet breakdowns.

Conclusions

Trade protectionist barriers are mainly practiced at the borders to shelter domestic producers and local businesses from stiff international competition. The most common types of protectionist features that occur at the borders involve tariff and non-tariff barriers. The application of exorbitant import tariffs acts as a measure to discourage or prohibit external suppliers to supply their goods and services since high tariff rates adversely impact on profitability. However, the increasing intensity of regional integration has resulted in the elimination and reduction of tariff rates and this has eroded the impact of tariff barriers thereby contributing to the emergence of harmful trade barriers referred to as NTBs (Angwenyi, 2014). The most common types of NTBs that were observed at Zimbabwe's borders include: border delays, use of outdated technology, lack of modern signage, corruption, physical and mental harassment, unnecessary inspections and searches, outdated technology, bureaucratic pathology, existence of unnecessary border agencies and harassment (physical, psychological and mental) of traders. Generally, border protectionism has several negative effects such as retaliation by neighbouring countries; long queues at the borders; congestion at the borders and the scaring away of potential foreign investors. Local consumers are restricted to local products only given the lack of competition in the domestic markets.

It has been noted in this chapter that border management is one of the most significant aspects of a nation since it determines national security issues. Weak border management programmes usually lead to the nation's vulnerability to international threats like international terrorism, women trafficking, child trafficking, drug trafficking, and the economy will be under threat from international competitor companies. Thus, effective border management requires monitoring of goods and people entering and exiting a country. Border management is also used as an effective way of managing the national economy. Governments therefore impose some trade barriers at the border to protect their economy from international threats. The major programmes implemented at the Zimbabwean borders to address trade barriers at the same time enhancing trade facilitation include BEMS, OSBP, IBM and ASYCUDA. COMESA as a regional organisation has promoted the successful implementation of the highlighted programmes through: supporting research, funding, enhancing capacity building programmes and liaising with cooperating partners, among others. This study noted that these programmes are effective in addressing border trade protectionism.

The major challenges affecting Zimbabwe's border management programmes are poor infrastructure, the dependency syndrome, bureaucracy, globalisation, lack of research, lack of Memoranda of Understanding entered into by the government to enhance border management, the prevalence of bogus border agencies since no authority has been appointed to direct operations at the borders, the absence of a Border Act and the individualism among border agencies. The basic strategies that should be implemented to improve border management in Zimbabwe are: investing in research, application of automation technology to all border agencies, introduction of a help desk at Zimbabwe's borders, improving internet connectivity at the ports of entry, appointing an authority or department to oversee and monitor border operations. The study, therefore, suggests that the implementation of these strategies could help improve the flow of goods across the borders thereby increasing the rate of trade liberalisation. The next chapter discusses the effects of trade protectionism on food security.

The border management and the ineffectiveness of border management such as ASYCUDA have a lot to do with the very weak political economy of Zimbabwe. The failure of Zimbabwe's economy to absorb the labour force and to efficiently produce enough goods and services for its citizens has contributed to the exodus of Zimbabweans to neighbouring countries such as South Africa which is estimated to be hosting about two million people. This exodus has increased pressure on the Beitbridge border post. Such as the congestion and subsequently the establishment of environment that breed corruption. A general economic malaise has also forced the ZIMRA officers to solicit bribes from travellers and traders. Dealing with this rampant corruption has been an Achilles' heel for the ZIMRA.

According to this study, effectiveness of ASYCUDA requires a combination of robust strategies from different angles, including political will, massive educational awareness, addressing remuneration of customs officials and effective law enforcement, complemented with an effective justice system. More importantly, the implementation of anti-corruption strategies such as the automation of systems and the mounting of highway patrols should be effectively conducted to reduce and eradicate corruption. However, although the ZIMRA has tried all these initiatives, effectiveness of ASYCUDA in managing borders in Zimbabwe is still a challenge, as indicated by high levels of smuggling occurring at Zimbabwe's border posts.

The study indicates that Zimbabwe's major impediments to optimal revenue collection at border posts include corruption which manifests itself in smuggling and bribes facilitated by revenue officials and touts. Although the ZIMRA customs unit has enough border management strategies like ASYCUDA in its toolkit, there is a serious problem with implementation, while corruption has continued unabated. It is evident that the effectiveness of ASYCUDA can be contained by current anti-corruption strategies if the ZIMRA could clearly integrate its operational mandate with other anti-corruption agents. However, this will also require an optimal political economy environment that will provide a strong base for anti-corruption initiatives.

The huge amount of poverty in Zimbabwe is the main driving force behind corruption and a main hindrance undermining the effectiveness of ASYCUDA. In as much as ZIMRA has enough strategies to combat corruption, poverty levels have severely weakened these strategies and rendered them virtually useless. Traders smuggle goods for survival hence it is not easy to deal with such perverse activities as long as they are driven by poverty and the need to survive. A combination of congestion and poor sanitary facilities within the border precincts all contribute to an environment conducive for the emergence and development of corruption. In order to address corruption, issues of congestion and sanitation will have to be tackled first.

Recommendations

The following recommendations are made by way of re-emphasising some important things that the ZIMRA needs do in order to enhance the effectiveness of ASYCUDA and border management in Zimbabwe:

- Restructuring of the ZIMRA management and rotating the station of operation to avoid creation of accomplices.
- Improving internet connectivity at the border posts
- The government should offer effective training facilities to Zimbabwean traders so that they may have a better understanding of ASYCUDA.
- ZIMRA should offer periodic workshops and training programmes to its officers so that they can adapt to the dynamic nature of trade facilitation and ASYCUDA.

Reference

Ayres, I. & Braithwaite, J. (1992). Responsive regulation: Transcending the deregulation debate. New York: Oxford University Press.

Angwenyi, V. 2014. Competition Law and Regional Integration: The Common Market for Eastern and Southern Africa (COMESA). Munich: Ludwig-Maximilians University.

Asian Development Bank, 2013. Modernising Sanitary and Phytosanitary Measures to Facilitate Trade in Agricultural and Food Products. Mandaluyong: Asian Development Bank.

Automated System for Customs Data (ASYCUDA), 2017. Accessed 5 June 2017, from www.asycuds.org/awintro.asp.

Baldwid, R. 2014. Multilateralising 21st Century Regionalism. Geneva: OECD.

Bernard, H.R. 2002. Research Methods in Anthropology: Qualitative and QuantitativeMethods, California: Altamira Press.

Bhagwati, J. 2002. *In Defence of Globalization*. London: Oxford University Press.

Bjelic, P. 2011. Non-Tariff Barriers as Obstacles to CEFTA Interregional Trade. Skopje: Institute of Economics.

Bloch, A., Seale, C., and Phellas, N.C. 2011. *Structured Methods: Interviews, Questionnaires and Observations.* London: Sage Publications.

Creswell, J.W. (1998). Qualitative inquiry and research design: Choosing among five traditions. Thousand Oaks, CA: Sage.

Creswell, J.W. (2003). Research design: Qualitative, quantitative, and mixed methods approaches. (2nd ed.). Thousand Oaks, CA: Sage

ESCAP (United Nations Economic and Social Commission for Asia and the Pacific). (2004). ESCAP trade facilitation framework: A guiding tool. New York: United Nations.

ESCAP (United Nations Economic and Social Commission for Asia and the Pacific). (2006). Trade facilitation and the new security environment: Issues for developing and least developed countries in the Asian and Pacific Region. Committee on Managing Globalization. 3rd session, 12-14 September 2006.

Mikuriya, K. (2005). Legal framework for customs operations and enforcement issues. In L. De Wulf & J. Sokol (Eds.), Customs modernization handbook (pp.31-50). Washington, DC: World Bank.

Messerlin, P.A. & Zarrouk, J. (2000). Trade facilitation: Technical regulations and customs procedures. World Economy, 23(4), 577-593.

Esterberg, K.G. (2002). Qualitative methods in social research. Boston, MA: McGraw-Hill.

Taneja, N. (2004). Trade facilitation in the WTO: Implications for India. Working Paper No.128. Indian Council for Research on International Economic Relations, New Delhi

Chirisa, I. 2013. Housing and Stewardship in Peri-Urban Settlement in Zimbabwe: A Case Study of Ruwa and Epworth. Harare: University of Zimbabwe.

Churchill, G.A. 2009. *Marketing Research: Methodological Foundations.* London: Dryden Press.

Colman, D. 2001. The Common Agricultural Policy: In the Economics of the European Union. New York: Oxford University Press.

COMESA, 2010a. Report on the Twenty Ninth Meeting of the Council of Ministers. Theme: Harnessing Science and Technology for Development. Lusaka: COMESA

COMESA, 2010b. Trade Facilitation Study in COMESA: Pilot Case Study on COMESA Sub-region. Lusaka: COMESA

COMESA, 2011. Harnessing Science and Technology for development. Lusaka. COMESA.

COMESA, 2012. Report of the Twenty Eight Meeting of the Trade and Customs Committee. 18-20 July 2012. Lusaka COMESA.

COMESA, 2013a: *International Trade statistics.* Lusaka: COMESA

Cresswell, J.W. 2012. Planning, Conducting and Evaluating Quantitative and Qualitative Research. Madrid: Pearson.

Creswell, J. 2003. Research Design, Qualitative, Quantitative and Mixed Methods Approaches: London: Sage Publications.

Creswell, J.W. 2009. Research Design: Qualitative, Quantitative and Mixed Methods Approaches. London: Sage Publications.

Denzin, N. 1970. *The Research Act in Sociology.* Chicago: Aldine.

Doyle, T., Fanta, E., Mclinden, G., and Widdowson, D. 2011. *Border Management Modernisation.* Washington: Word Bank.

Draper, P. 2012. *Competitiveness, Protectionism, and the WTO.* Johannesburg: South Africa Institute of International Affairs.

Drew, S., Cox, S., and Warr, D. 2014. *Guideline for Ethical Visual Research Methods.* Melbourne: University of Melbourne.

Drope, J. 2011. Tobacco control in Africa: People Politics and Policies, London: Arithem Press.

Dube, C and Ngoma, S. 2012. Aid for Trade and Economic Development : A Case Study of Zambia. Lusaka: CUTS international.

Erasmus, G. 2013. The COMESA Court of Justice: Regional Agreements Do Protect Private Parties. Stellenbosch: Trade Law Centre

Friedman, T. 2006. The world is flat: The Globalised world in the 20th century London: Penguin

Fugazza, M. 2010. The Impact of Removal of ATC Quotas on International Trade in Textile and Apparel. Geneva: United Nations Conference on Trade and Development.

Mubaiwa, S. 2013. An Evaluation of Trade Facilitation Measures Implemented by the Common Market for Eastern and Southern Africa (COMESA): The Case of Chirundu One Stop Border Post. Bindura: Bindura University of Science and Education.

Nkwemu, M. 2011. The One Stop Border Concept: A Case of Chirundu Border Post Between Zambia and Zimbabwe. Lusaka: Government of Zambia.

Shalizi, R.C. 2015. Advanced Data Analysis from an Elementary Point of View. California: spring.

Silva, D. 2013. Trade Facilitation: Identifying Opportunities Through Afghanistan WTO Accession and Membership. Bangkok: ESCAP.

United Nations, 2011a. *Technical Notes on Trade Facilitation Measures.* Geneva: United Nations Conference on Trade and Development.

Zhou, G. 2006. An Analysis of the Objectives and Effects of Privatisation on the Private Sector Role of the State in Zimbabwe. Harare: Zimbabwe Coalition on Debt and Development.

CHAPTER SIX

The nexus between
Security and Border Management in Zimbabwe:
The case of Beitbridge Border Post

Charity Manyeruke

Introduction

The issue of border security and management is very crucial in Africa as it relates to economic development of countries. Scholars have argued that in the wake of technology and globalization, there is need to embrace the two in order to curb various security threats rocking borders in Africa. Barka (2012:10) defines the border as: "a location where one country's authority over goods and persons ends and another country's authority begin." Due to the fact that it involves both livelihood of both ordinary citizens and even the government (from revenue) the issue of security and border management thus becomes critical.

Border security can be defined as the awareness of the border that effectively thwarts the ability of the criminal elements to operate. The aim is to reduce the vulnerability (chaos and clutter) of an uncontrolled border so as to improve the quality of life for the residents and legitimate businesses and reduce the risk to the nation's economic vitality (Manjarezz 2015). Various scholars have argued that most African countries are losing a lot of revenue due to the fact that their borders are too porous and lack proper management. This is the main highlight at the Beitbridge border post.

A lot of criminal activities have characterized the Beitbridge border post and these include human and goods smuggling, human trafficking, corruption by border officials, arms smuggling and sexual harassment. Much needs to be done as far as security and management is concerned. The report on human smuggling across the South Africa /Zimbabwe Border (2009:5) postulates that, human smugglers are able to charge high fees for their services and in a number of cases, abuse their clients by extorting money from them or abandoning them in dangerous environments. This has been reportedly the case at the Beitbridge border post and clearly it shows that the level of security that is in existence at the moment need an upgrade which can be either in addition of more personnel or improving on science and technology.

Therefore this chapter seeks to highlight the challenges that are being faced at the Beitbridge border post as far as security is concerned. The other important aspect that the study seeks to address is to give recommendations to the current security challenges faced at the border post.

Security and Management: Historical Background

Security has always been a very important subject particularly with reference to the border posts as it involves national interests. Nations have always wanted to control what goes in and out of their countries as this allows them to maintain a certain level of power. The areas that have been of concern since back then have been drug and human smuggling, the illegal entrance of people in a state. The report on human smuggling across the South Africa/ Zimbabwe border (2009: 3) argues that, human smuggling is different from human trafficking because human trafficking involves from the outset, an intention by the trafficker to profit from the forced exploitation (for instance through sex, servitude or slavery) of the persons smuggled illegally. The Southern African Development Community (2011:14) states that, responsibility for protecting state's interests is vested in several state agencies. The state agents include the police, state security, the customs, immigration, those responsible for sanitary (relating to human and animal products) and phyto sanitary (relating to plant products) regulations and the bureau standards. The responsibility of security on the state is to ensure that resources are properly allocated to ensure the safety of citizens and the nation at large. After the wake of the September 11 attack on America by terrorist groups, the security on borders has especially been tightened to try and protect counties interests.

Scholars have been interested in how the border is manned and also the fact that who actually do the management of the agencies stationed at the border. Some of the major weaknesses being faced at the border are as a result that there is poor management which may lead to the duplication of duties. Proper coordination of different stakeholders is important to ensure the effective delivery of services. Irish (2005:8) points out that, apart from insufficient coordination between different departments stationed at the border, there are also weaknesses in the system used to detect vehicles being smuggled through the border post. This shows that much still needs to be done in the area of border management.

Theoretical Framework

Territorial Indivisibility

Gavrilis (2006:8) highlights that, one possible explanation to the subject of border security comes from the literature on territorial indivisibility. Much of this work argues that most modern inter-state conflict is not based on a struggle for power or survival. Instead, states fight over territory. The main argument in this theory is that states feel the need to protect their territories through border security. The presence of uniformed forces like the Zimbabwe National Army and Zimbabwe Republic Police at the Beitbridge border post is an indication that all forms of security threats need to be guarded against. It is because states always find themselves disputing over various issues because in the absence of territorial disputes, we should see permissive conditions for cross-border cooperation and joint policing.

After the September 11 attack on the United States of America, most nations have been vigilant on border security. More stringent requirements are now a must for one to cross the border from one nation to the other. The exiting of the European Union by United Kingdom can also better explain the territorial indivisibility. States feel the need to protect their identity and people by protecting their borders. Security traditionally has been perceived as the physical presence of armed forces but with the wake of globalization new meanings have been drawn on this subject.

A Theory of State-building and Border Security

State-building refers to the attempt by states to expand political authority and monopoly of rule over their territory. In other words, border control strategies are generated from the inside-out and not from objective threat emanating from the international environment. Gavrilis (2006: 11) is of the assumption that, all states desire secure boundaries. States may deploy a variety of strategies along their borders in order to accomplish their preferred tasks. These strategies may include militarization and deployment of combat units, stationing of professional border guards, construction of physical barriers or the use of high-tech tools to process the flow of movement in and out of Zimbabwe. On this note Gavrilis was emphasizing the fact that it is important for any country to secure its borders by any means possible. Zimbabwe is no one country that is an exception. The Beitbridge border post is one example of how the government is trying to regulate on whom and what comes in and out of the country.

Still on the issue of theory of state building and security, Gavrilis (2006: 11) asserts that, as institutions that delineate the end of one state's sovereignty and the beginning of another, borders allow states to extend their authority to defined lines with the promise of non-interference from the outside. However, borders are more than reminders of the sovereignty norm. They are also local level institutions where states may choose to physically perform tasks to further their aims of state building or reaffirm their sovereignty. Customs officials who tax goods, border guards who patrol against illegal entry and exit, and combat units that act as lines of first defense are such examples of state building and sovereignty.

Literature Review

Border security and management has always been regarded as an area of importance for decades. However after the attack on America by terrorist groups and also new regulations from the World Trade Organization made countries tighten their security on the border. The other reason for tightened security is that with constant advancement in science and technology, the mobility of people from one country to the other has increased putting national security of states to be compromised in a number of ways. A Homeland Security Report (2015:6) states that, at ports of entry in the year 2015, the Customs and Border Protection officers arrested 8,246 individuals wanted for serious crimes. Officers also stopped 225,342 inadmissible individuals from entering the United States through ports of entry, an increase of 14 percent from the year 2014. These individuals were deemed inadmissible for a variety of reasons, including immigration violations, criminal and other violations, and national security reasons. Depending on the circumstances, these individuals were arrested, allowed to voluntarily return to their Country of origin, or allowed to withdraw their application for admission into the United States.

Provision of Security at the Beitbridge Border Post

Several security agencies provide security at the Beitbridge border post, with the government being the major provider of security. Irish (2005: 10) asserts that, the various agencies providing security at the Beitbridge border include:

- Zimbabwe Revenue Authority (ZIMRA).
- Department of Immigration control.
- Ministry of Agriculture- Plant Protection Inspectorate.
- Ministry of Agriculture- Vet Inspectorate.
- Ministry of Health- Port Health Inspectorate.
- Medicines Control Authority of Zimbabwe (MCAZ).
- Zimbabwe Republic Police (ZRP).
- ZRP Border Control Unit.
- Central Intelligence Office (CIO).
- Ministry of Transport: Vehicle Inspectorate Department (VID).
- Environmental Management Agency (EMA).
- Zimbabwe National Army (ZNA).

The complex nature of the security needed at the border requires a number of agencies as can be seen from the above. For instance the Ministry of Agriculture ensures that no plants or animals that are not approved nor have proper documentation are allowed into the country. The fact that security covers a lot of aspects, then follows that if not properly managed it can be compromised.

The state has a huge interest on the activities that take place at the border. State interests at the border include protection of national security, enforcement of immigration requirements, enforcement of import and export restrictions and prohibitions, collection of revenue, recording cross border statistics and enforcement of sanitary and phyto sanitary measures and technical standards (SADC 2011). Clearly the duty of providing security at the border solely rests with the state.

Role played by Security agents at the Border

Border control covers both irregular and illegal entry, and legal entry. The first kind of border control is preventive policing and involves the apprehension of illegal migrants and traffickers at borders and will usually involve surveillance and patrolling activity of some kind. The Zimbabwe Republic Police (ZRP) as well as the Zimbabwe National Army (ZNA) play the role of patrolling the Beitbridge border post to ensure that illegal immigrants do not enter into the country and also making sure that a number of security issues are being followed as per protocol procedures for citizens both entering into Zimbabwe as well as leaving the country. On the subject of the roles done by security agencies, Shayanowako (2013: 13) argues that, ZRP, CIO , Immigration Control and ZNA are concerned with national and public order and security, there should be need for cooperation in the discharge of their roles in a manner that facilitates a coordinated, smooth and expeditious movement of people and goods across the border.

The maintenance of peace and order is also a critical role played by security agents and also the role of deterrence to any criminal activities that would instead taken place had they not been there. Henry (2010:8) argues that the conceptual model of border security described in the preceding section highlights three core functions of border-security operations: (1) interdiction, (2) deterrence, and (3) exploitation of networked intelligence. In other words the scholar was highlighting that in the United States of America the police have an important role in the areas of deterrence.

According to Irish (2005:3) the National Intelligence from the South African side plays the role of patrolling and securing the border, home affairs department playing the role of dealing with the movement of people across the border. The major question therefore is that despite all the security officers at the border who exactly is responsible for controlling access to the border control area. That role is not clearly defined. However even though the uniformed forces play an important role on upholding peace at the border a number of cases have been reported that have compromised the role they are supposed to play. Toy (2011:15) argues that most of the sexual harassment offences at the Beitbridge border post are committed by officials (customs officials, police and soldiers). Reports like these show how a lot still needs to be done at the border to ensure that travelers are not intimidated and also to embrace modern technology that also allow for the border to be monitored at all times. Matakanye (2011:12) still on the issue of harassment further highlighted that, an average 10 women are raped on the South African border daily. Such reports shows that not much is being done to ensure that the safety of citizens.

Activities that compromise Security at Border

The Zimbabwe/ South African border post has been dubbed by several scholars as a hub of activities because of the amount of trucks and citizens that the border post deals with on a daily basis. Chiliya (2014: 16) points out that, a border is a facility that provides controlled entry in and out of any country, usually accommodating customs and immigration, as well as other inspection agencies responsible for enforcement of that country's laws. Because the law has to be enforced at all times it means the activities at the border need to be managed critically. Beitbridge border post is one of the most porous border posts in Zimbabwe. People could be seen entering and leaving the border without proper searches or declarations (Munyanyi 2015). Already it shows the loophole at the Beitbridge border post because if people could enter and leave without proper documentation check it shows that so much needs attention.

Barka (2012:4) highlights that, the inadequate and poor quality of transportation infrastructure in African countries acts as a major hindrance to the free flow of goods across borders .Given the substandard condition of the African road network (only 22.7 percentis currently paved), the poor interconnectivity of the rail networks, and the limited capacity of many smaller ports to accommodate the largest supersize container ships, moving goods across borders is very costly and subject to lengthy delays. This is especially linked to the Beitbridge border post where travellers and travel agents refer to it as a norm for one person to spend a few hours by the border just to get their passport stamped. A Zimbabwe Revenue Authority official who preferred anonymity argued that especially during holidays like Christmas and Easter, the Beitbridge border post can deter business persons who would have cargo that needs to be ferried in or out of Zimbabwe. The situation was described as very bad to the extent that cars and people could be seen queuing with little progress at the counters.

The haphazard parking of cars at the Beitbridge border is another activity that poses security challenges. According to Chiliya (2014:22),

The existence of ranking facilities at various border entrances in the SADC region where taxis (many which do not have cross-border permits) rank to offload and load cross border passengers, disrupt traffic movements at border posts. Apart from aggravating congestion at border posts, this practice also compromises border control operations, security and integrity. Furthermore it exacerbates and creates opportunities for criminal activities such as smuggling and robbery.

The confusion created by these taxi operators could be intentional just so that the security agents as well as other officials would not be able to tell as to who is legal or not. The other side could be that some of officials are part of the underhand dealings that would be going on with the same taxi operators.

Ettienne (1998: 130 argues that, crime syndicates sometimes bribe police, customs immigration and other officials to turn a blind eye to crime at borders that involved the smuggling of drugs, cars, prostitutes, endangered species products and firearms across South Africa International borders. Even though this was documented long back an interview with various individuals who frequented the border confirmed it was common activity at the border for people to "jump" the border. In essence it is argued by several scholars that the people who facilitate the illegal entry of people in and out of countries will be working with security officers.

| Chapter Six | Charity Manyeruke |

Corruption and Security

Corruption at the Beitbridge border post is termed by scholars as one of the biggest challenges giving rise to a lot more problems coupled with the science and technology problem. The absence of closed circuit television (CCTV) or any electronic surveillance mechanism in place makes it very easy for corrupt activities to go unnoticed. It was observed that the border post is very busy at midday and midnight and, at these times, it is densely populated. Ettiene (1998:13) asserts that, corruption is another factor starting to become synonymous with border posts and officials responsible for border control activities. The other problem that is also allowing corruption to go to such levels is that people are not aware of where to report such criminal activities and those who know about it turn a blind eye and do not report it possibly because they have no trust in the system that anything would be done after the reports. As the transparency and predictability of trade and business administrations are lacking, most customs officers and companies/traders routinely find themselves engaged in bribery acts and the under-declaration of goods as means to "facilitate" payment (Barka 2012). Irish (2005:8) postulates that, the smuggling of vehicles across the border post is perceived to be entirely a police matter. There is little inter- departmental cooperation in this regard. As such if there is no proper delimitation of duties and roles it means the border may be neglected and also gives rise to corruption.

Coordination at the Border (Management)

The Southern African Development Community (2011:11) defines border management as national and international coordination and cooperation among all the relevant authorities and agencies involved in the protection of the interests of the state at the border to establish effective, efficient and coordinated border management in order to reach the objective of open but well controlled secure borders. The most important fact is that all the personnel at the border need to be coordinated and one scholar suggested that it would be even more manageable if there was one agency responsible for the management of the border.

The customs environment in the Southern and Eastern African sub-region is characterised by a lack of coordination among the multiple government agencies on both sides of borders which, in turn, increases the potential for fraud and the need for risk management (Barka 2012). Thus proper border management is very important. SADC (2011: 25) argues that, SADC member states should clarify which agency is responsible for border surveillance. Lack of clarity can lead to inter-agency rivalries, duplication of resources, illegal border crossing or lack of allocation of resources to border patrols.

Shayanowako (2013:7) further highlights that; border management can therefore be taken to comprise the systems, processes and procedures followed by or guiding a country's border agencies in ensuring the flow of traffic across the country's borders with other countries. This means there is a significant importance on how one country manages its borders. If not properly done then security becomes compromised. Thus efficient border management requires that there is cooperation of all border management agencies (ranging from security personnel to even the people who stamp passports) and such cooperation can be achieved if proper coordination mechanisms, legal framework and institutions are established. Shayanowako (2013:16) further posits that, there is no formal institutional framework established to coordinate and oversee border management efficiency programmes, as a result individual border agencies can only do what they consider reasonable- which may not amount to full cooperation with other agencies. The argument here is that even though security personnel might be enough to protect the country's interests, the agencies at these borders do not have a clear division of labor and sometimes it results in duplication of duties.

Information and Technology

The infrastructure shortcomings at Beitbridge border post present a breeding ground for illegal activities including smuggling. There is no proper modern technology that can allow the officials to be able to detect corruption and crime (PWC, 2015:8) argues that, Individuals identities have traditionally been verified by biographical information such as passports. But this data is only as accurate as the documentation presented, making identity fraud a key area of weakness for border management. The Beitbridge border has been a victim of this type of fraud. Due to the huge volumes of people and goods being moved at this border post it has been common practice for people to fake documentation. There is need to embrace science and technology and find new ways of dealing with modern crimes.

According to Fitzmaurice (2009: 6), the immigration and custom officials are very few, are very slow in serving people, spend a lot of time on their phones, harass travelers, do not control the queues, and take a lot of time when changing shifts. The analysis from this scholar shows that there is no proper management of personnel and activities that generally take place at the border. Another conclusion that can be drawn from this can be that there are no proper modern methods of science and technology being put in place or adopted. This has been a major cause of corruption and other crimes related to the border. The Homeland Security Report (2015: 7) highlights that, the Cross Border Protection in United States of America invested in eight Tethered Aerostat Radar Systems (TARS) which form a network of long-range radars deployed on the border. The TARS, which can identify and monitor low-altitude aircraft and vessels at a distance of 200 miles, increases domain awareness and provides personnel with critical additional time to assess and respond to possible incursions. The system recorded more than 335 suspected cross-border attempts in 2015, about 40 percent of all border-related radar detections. With the volume of traffic and people at the Beitbridge border post this is the type of technology advancement that is needed.

Conclusion

The subject of border security is very important to most nations as it defines a country's sovereignty as well as the protection of its nationals. In most African countries the most common border challenges are those of smuggling, human trafficking as well as the illegal entry of people in and out of countries with no proper documentation. The Beitbridge border post is one of the busiest borders in Southern Africa receiving large volumes of cargo as well as cross border traders going in and out of Zimbabwe. Scholars have argued that, the fact that the harsh economic conditions in Zimbabwe have forced a number of people to do cross border business. With the spread of globalization, states are facing new types of security challenges at the border. Proper management of security is important and requires the coordination of all security personnel.

Recommendations

- Munyanyi (2015:6) highlights that, it is imperative that all ports of entry be under constant surveillance to ensure that illegal activities are detected and measures to deter them are implemented in good time. It is also easy to identify syndicates when they are placed on computer-aided surveillance.

- Unmanned Aircraft Surveillance can also be used at the border to detect illegal activities. The Homeland Security Report (2015:8) stipulates that, in addition, Air and Marine Operations has deployed two Unmanned Aircraft Systems along the Southwest Border in America to detect, identify and classify moving tracks of interest over land. These systems are equipped with Vehicle and Dismount Exploitation Radar, a side-looking airborne radar that has the capability to relay real-time tactical information related to illegal cross-border activity to field agents while simultaneously capturing strategic and forensic information across larger stretches of the border. With this system it would be easy to detect illegal and corrupt activities happening at the border.

- In addition, the parking bays for commercial vehicles need to be improved to enable effective surveillance. Disorganized and random parking encourages illegal activities through reduced visibility.

- Barka (2012:6) asserts that the lengthy procedures for clearing goods at border posts could be addressed by the introduction of comprehensive automated systems for document checking and clearing. Many African border posts do not use modern information technology in domestic and international trade. Barka (2012:7) argues that, for instance, in Angola, the efficient use of modern information technologies for customs procedures has significantly cut processing time and increased customs revenues by 150 percent.

References

Barka, H. 2012. Border posts, checkpoints, and Intra African Trade: Challenges and Solutions. Switzerland. Echandens.

Chiliya, N. 2014. Challenges facing Zimbabwean cross border traders trading in South Africa: A review of literature. South Africa. Monash University.

Ettienne, H. 1998. The challenges to control South Africa's borders and borderline. Ethiopia. Dilla University.

Fitzmaurice, M. 2009. Situational analysis at Beitbridge border post between Zimbabwe and South Africa. Johannesburg. Transport Logistics Consultants.

Gavrilis, G. 2006. Policing the Periphery: A theory of border control from the Central Asian Context. Austin. University of Texas.

Henry, H. 2010. *Measuring the effectiveness of border security between ports of entry*. Santa Monica. Homeland Security and defense center

Human smuggling report across the South Africa/ Zimbabwe border. 2009. Human smuggling. South Africa. Witwatersrand.

Homeland Security Report. 2015. *CBP Border Security Report*. USA. US Customs and Border Protection.

Irish, J. 2005. *Illicit trafficking of vehicles across Beitbridge border post*. South Africa. Institute of Security Studies.

Kwanisai, G. 2014. Borders as barriers to tourism: tourists experience at the Beitbridge border post (Zimbabwean side). Chinhoyi. African journal of hospitality.

Manjarezz, V. 2015. Border Security: Defining it is the real challenge. USA.University of Texas.

Matakanye, J. 2011. *Raped on SA border daily*. http://www.newzimbabwe

Munyanyi, W. 2015. Is Infrastructure upgrading an antidote for smuggling? Evidence from Beitbridge Border Post, Zimbabwe. Zimbabwe.World Customs Journal.

Shayanowako, P. 2013. Study into the cooperation of border management agencies in Zimbabwe. Stellenbosch. Tralac

Southern African Development Community. 2011. *SADC draft guidelines for coordinated border management*. Gaborone. SADC.

Toy, J. 2011. *Beitridge border post: the challenges.* South Africa. University of
    Pretoria.
www.pwc.com The future of border management: Maintaining security,
    facilitating and prosperity

Chapter Seven

Drug trafficking, Drug Laws and Border Control in Zimbabwe: Multidisciplinary Analysis for Zimbabwe?

Sharon Hofisi

Introduction

This chapter first appeared as a newspaper article in the Herald under the title, '*War on Drugs: Normative viewpoints*' (Hofisi 2017). What touched off this expanded academic chapter is obviously the pleasure that was raised by the original article among academics and avid readers. The feedback and discussions between this author and academic colleagues as well as students at the University of Zimbabwe justified the need to broaden the reach of this chapter to students of international relations, democracy and human rights and international law and the general Zimbabwean populace at large. As such, a scoping analysis of the drug-problem responses is given in this chapter. The chapter examines how civil society organizations (CSOs) collaborate with the Government of Zimbabwe to ensure that Zimbabwe's border policies and law enforcement mechanisms address the drug problem effectively beyond the rubric of 'War on drugs'. The approach adopted in this paper is based on the United Nations' (UN) definition on drug trafficking to include the cultivation, manufacturing, distribution and sale of illicit drugs. It however draws on lessons from studies on how sub-regions like West-Africa have encouraged collaboration between CSOs and government to reduce harm caused by drugs such as cocaine.

Broadly speaking, Zimbabwe was considered in this think piece to be a source, transit zone as well as destination for illicit drugs. As a source, illicit brews such as *Kachasu or nipa (home made amarula), chikokiyana/Chikw akubidhiri (one-day brew)* and prescription drugs such as broncleer that are manufactured in countries like South Africa and are smuggled through the Beitbridge border post are examined from the perspective of their health implications on Zimbabweans. As a transit zone and destination for illicit drugs, this chapter examined how the porosity of Zimbabwe's borders is contributing to the smuggling of drugs. These drugs find their way into the central border district of Zimbabwe's capital, Harare, and into most high density suburbs where urban youths end up being the biggest consumers. As such, the subject of this chapter was to examine the relationship between drug trafficking and border control mechanisms on the one hand and to signpost response strategies on the part of government and CSOs on the other. The analysis took consideration of the controversies that surround the use of prescription drugs, home-made alcoholic beverages, as well as conventional illicit drugs. As the second part of the title of this article suggests, an effort was made to find the role of a multi-sector approach in dealing with issues such as criminality, decriminalization, policy formulation and policy implementat ion and so forth. The chapter found that *if* Zimbabwe is to carve lasting solutions to its drug problems, *then* it has to adopt an integrated approach where stakeholders are informed both by the local norms and laws on the one hand, and international norms on the other.

The chapter also focused on the growing international need to treat both drugs themselves and drug laws as part of the bigger drug problem that is tearing apart the social fabric of societies the world over. There are issues to deal with traditional uses of drugs, drug laws which are used to impose lengthy prison terms on users and manufacturers and the drug regulatory framework which is not usually debated in public platforms for the benefit of the greater public. In asking whether or not drug trafficking can be curbed in Zimbabwe, this chapter argued that a country-specific study such as this, ought to come to grips with the frequently asked questions as to *what kind of drugs are being trafficked to and from Zimbabwe? What causes the most social damage, drugs themselves or drug laws? How does the furor on drugs and border concerns illuminate how Zimbabwe's drug policy is affecting the border control mechanisms in the affected countries such as Mozambique, Zambia, and South Africa?*

While the answers to the first two questions above may be obtained from the various sections of the Zimbabwean society which have been affected by the drug problem, the answer to the third question helps researchers and policy framers to locate the fight against illicit drugs as not only requiring a lot of resources-both human and material, but requiring Zimbabweans to appreciate the opaque and controversial aspects surrounding drug trafficking. Ideally, this calls for an inclusive approach to solving the drug problem. Actually, in this social milieu, the real problems and effects of illicit drugs on the Zimbabwean society have to be considered by looking at the role of laws and organizations involved in fighting the use of illicit drugs. The base on knowledge and information-sharing between policy framers/researchers and the users or players in the game has to be broadened if a rational and largely riskless approach is to be designed in Zimbabwe.

Statement of the problem

The leading concern in this article is that if effective border management is done properly and collaboratively by immigration officials, researchers, CSOs, and other government institutions, the effect of social resistance to the drug-problem can yield positive changes for Zimbabwe. Furthermore, the social resistance will continue on the part of those who appreciate that drug trafficking at Zimbabwean borders is rampant. Poor border management is the major reason why drugs either enter or leave Zimbabwe, mainly as a result of the activities of cross border traders and drivers of haulage trucks (Chipunza and Razemba 2017). Zimbabwe does not have a flexible domestic drug policy which can curb the cultivation, manufacture, distribution or sale of illicit drugs within Zimbabwe. To that extent, it can remain a source of illicit drugs, some of which are never sold to other countries. Further, Zimbabwe is a destination and transit zone for illicit drugs which are trafficked by both foreigners and Zimbabwean citizens through both the major borders and the smaller borders. In this wake, border leakages have to be addressed in light of the international outcry on the increase in global illicit drugs such as cocaine and marijuana. Zimbabwe's drug laws must be reformed or aligned with the Constitution so that a culture of impunity is changed through decriminalization, consideration of traditional and religious beliefs and so forth which augur well with the spirit of the constitution. In doing so, this article proposed a sound theory of rights and responsibilities which starts from placing emphasis on the norms of the various peoples who form part of the Zimbabwean society. The proposed theory is meant to enable CSOs, researchers and policy makers to appreciate the emerging normative framework at both the national and international legal levels. Norms largely allow for tolerance between societies as well as encouraging such societies to participate in the governance programs that affect them.

Setting the pillars for argumentation

Drug Trafficking has been defined by the United Nations Office of Drugs and Crime (UNODC) (2018) as:

> A global illicit trade involving the cultivation, manufacture, distribution and sale of substances which are subject to drug prohibition laws *(underlining intentionally made)*.

Four important aspects of the UNODC definition have to be considered at the very outset to show why Zimbabwe is the source of illicit drugs: Cultivation; manufacture; distribution and sale of substances. Zimbabweans have been found on the wrong side of the law for cultivating *muzii/mbanje/chamba/dobho/weed* (marijuana/Nigerian grass/G anja in some circles). Some manufacture illicit brews using local plants such as corn, sorghum, millet, finger millet, *marula* fruit/jelly plum (*mapfura* in Shona/*umganu* in Ndebele) and *masau (Ziziphus mauritiana)*. While marijuana is believed to be part of hair food, or herbal tool to scare away witches and spooks, Jelly plum is used to prepare wine (*mukumbi*) whose alcohol content is not known. The failure to ascertain content has delirious effects on the health of consumers. Marijuana is distributed and sold mainly to smokers. People smoke marijuana for various reasons including chasing away evil spirits, belief in Rastafarianism, extant myths on how marijuana increases one's mathematical intelligence, need to reduce stress, peer pressure, need for Dutch courage, addiction and so forth. There are writings on the other uses of the plum plant which include making plum oil, and skin ointments (Ngomani, 2016). Besides *mukumb*i, other local brews that are distributed and sold locally include *kachasu/nipa/chikokiyana/tototo and musombodhiya*. The health effects of such illicit brews are quite frightening considering that consumers and manufacturers are not aware of the alcohol content in the drugs they use or in the illicit brews they consume.

To that extent, the illicit brews are regarded as drugs because of their unascertained alcohol content.

Concerns on illicit brews include the need to determine the microbiological properties of the *Masau* fruit and the fermented pulp. Such concerns are considered important in selecting and possibly developing starter cultures for improved fermentation processes. In some studies carried out Zimbabwe, it was found the ethanol content of the fermented fruit pulp ranged from $2.1 - 3.7$ mL 100mL^{-1}, whereas the traditionally made distillate contained $23.8 - 45.6$ mL 100 mL^{-1} (Nyanga et al, 2008). This article took cognizance of the fact that there is paucity in official literature on how CSOs and the Zimbabwean government are collaborating to deal with drug trafficking and to campaign for the reduction of drug harm on the Zimbabwean urban and rural society. Generally most Zimbabweans are conservative and do not want intruders into their personal or societal lives, including reasons why they consume drugs. Even counselors, medical practitioners, families and other social institutions such as churches, youth clubs and so forth find it difficult to reach out to the affected age groups. Added to this is the fact that drug use in Zimbabwe has also been linked to crime (Tsakiwa 2012). Those who are willing to share their experiences usually do so through social media platforms such as radios, outside broadcasters and newspapers. The chapter took the stance that it is difficult to successfully talk about sensitive issues without, at the same time, considering the values of the various peoples and oversight institutions which work with drug users, or those found to be in conflict with the law.

Methodology

This chapter used an exploratory study design. Documentary search was done and the reviewed documents include textbooks, journal articles and newspaper articles. For instance, newspaper articles by investigative journalists were used to assess how illicit drugs have been smuggled through major border posts such as Nyamapanda and Beitbridge. The chapter also visited the Zimbabwe Revenue Authority (ZIMRA) webpage to determine how the nation's tax collector is helping government to curb corruption at border posts as well as curbing the flow of illicit drugs. Documentary review was also used to identify the common destinations of illicit drugs in Zimbabwe and beyond its borders. It was also observed in this study that media practitioners can sometimes obtain information about drugs from official websites of organizations such as the South African Police. As such, issues to do with professional ethics were found to be crucial in assessing how media practitioners gather information to be relayed to members of the public. Literature on other countries such as Mexico or the United States of America (USA) or from sub-regional drug responses was also reviewed to determine the extent of the drug problem at a global and continental level.

The literature from newspapers was not reviewed immensely because the identities of the drug users were mostly not revealed in some articles. Media practitioners normally ascribed pseudonyms to the users and the media practitioners often dissociated themselves from the information provided by the users by simply claiming that most of the supplied information would not have been verified. The articles were however considered to be reflective of the real situations which must be considered in crafting a theory of change in the attitudes of the target population: urban (mainly high density suburbs and peri-urban communities) and rural (including farming or mining communities and communities in Zimbabwe who brew illicit beer as well as traffickers who include Zimbabweans and non-Zimbabweans. The data collected were analyzed by grouping into themes and by analyzing various themes such as misuse of prescriptions, lack of determination of the alcohol content, ancillary criminal activities, motivating factors, decriminalization efforts and so on.

Theoretical framework

It was found in this chapter that effective country responses to drug problem do not happen overnight. A sound theory of rights and responsibilities is needed which is steeped in the constitutional gains that include freedom of conscience or religion, freedom of trade, occupation and profession. The use of this theory enables the local population to improve their lives by collaborating to resist social problems and by striving to design innovative ways of enhancing social development within communities. CSOs, academic researchers, policy framers and takers can unite in emancipating and empowering the locals to use local plants and resources for other development-oriented purposes other than for illicit brews or impulsive consumption of such brews. This sound theory of rights and responsibilities was informed by the normative framework espoused by the Constitution of Zimbabwe, 2013. Put differently, a Constitution is the Grundnorm or highest norm that guides a society on what values it cherishes for the greater benefit or common good of today's and tomorrow's generations.

In essence, the total context of this think piece was seen as a call for a normative framework to be established in dealing with the seemingly endemic and increasing drug problem in Zimbabwe. The Constitution allows stakeholders to posit the values of the feeder societies, which are also the distributing and consuming societies of illicit drugs. The normative framework under the constitution and the international framework under the United Nations (UN) were used to explain the relationship between local challenges and international challenges posed by drug trafficking and porous borders. The most important features under both frameworks were the need to prevent illicit drug leakages at borders and to transform the culture of locals from embedding their livelihoods in illicit drugs to the need to adopt a variegated approach which uses resources sustainably and for the betterment of society through innovative means.

Why Using Normative Theory as the working theory?

As it seems that the drug problem is endemic the world over, nations must make comprehensive arrangements in trying to avoid border leakages. The problems affecting nations are increasingly changing: organized violence, human trafficking, and trans-boundary conflicts and so on. Addressing drug problems in the age of power politics cannot only end on realism as a political theory which focuses on the ubiquity of politics. It can also not end on the need for States to concentrate on their survival in a polarized international community. To take only the justifications of political realism in this global problem, States would remain as the leading players in fighting drug trafficking. This is problematic since states normally define their national interests and areas of priority. And of course the significant role of non-governmental organizations (NGOs) and other non-State actors or social movements will be left out, much to the detriment of most societies where such organizations can play a significant role. The result, especially considering the rise of illegal use of banned drugs in most countries, is that States will habitually craft drug policies which only serve to exacerbate the drug problem than solve it.

The benefit of using an integrated norm-based approach allows both the targeted population of drug cultivators, manufacturers, distributors, sellers and consumers to assist the policy framers or regulators to include the *'ought to be'* of laws and policies. Making policies that end on legal positivism or the *'what it is'* of law yield no quick benefits to nations, especially when they fight a problem that has cartels, syndicates, and close communities. The law must not be overly used in a legalistic way to punish offenders without focusing on other deontologically using retribution consequentialist aspects such as reforming general deterrence or rehabilitating the offender. The other obvious justification for using the normative theory is that it allows researchers to focus on the utilitarian issues that are raised by various users and organizations which work with drug users. For instance, psychological issues such as behaviour proneness can assist researchers to focus on fundamental human rights to health as part of the founding values that are enshrined in section 3 of the Constitution of Zimbabwe, 2013 and design training programs that can be used to rehabilitate drug offenders as contemplated by the constitution. As the *Grundnorm*, the constitution enables various vulnerable groups to be emancipated and empowered using the constitutional values attached to the fundamental human rights of vulnerable and sometimes marginalized groups such as women, children, the youths, the elderly or people living with disabilities.

Moreover, those who deal with drug survivors or victors will use a human rights-based approach that is steeped in the need to uphold Zimbabwe's social norms. Sometimes drug victors may become victimisers. The constitution places duties on right holders and victimisers can be dealt with accordingly. Alternatively, sociological theories such as social control (which focuses on the need to promote bonds between the individual and the society) can be used together with the normative theory to enable researchers and policy framers to focus on the community values of various peoples or sections of the Zimbabwean society. At the end, Zimbabweans can gradually become aware of the constitutional provisions that have a normative content such as human rights, rights of women, children's rights, and the rule of law. Even biological control theories such as metabolic imbalance model will also take back the argument back to the Grundnorm on the norms such as the right to basic health care and limitations attached thereto. Essentially therefore, the policy framers and partner institutions ought to involve the public or CSOs in determining the motives for brewing illicit beers or growing, distribution and selling drugs such as marijuana. Participatory researches can be done so that research organizations can quantify the alcohol content in traditional brews such as *mukumbi, kachasu, or chikwakubhidhiri* (one-day brew). A sustainable culture of cooperation between the policy framer and policy taker can only be done through a value-based approach to solving endemic challenges.

At a national level, the constitution is the supreme or mother document which epitomizes the will of the diverse peoples in a polity. It also serves as a political or policy road map for the policy. Those who use *broncleer* (bronco in street language) for instance must be made aware that they cannot expect to be protected by the Constitution because *bronco* is not even licensed as a drug for medicinal use in Zimbabwe. Distributors and sellers can also be made aware of the criminal effects of their actions especially if regard is made to the health regulatory framework in Zimbabwe which prohibits the selling of such drugs. The absence of constitutional protection for some breaches on the law can be explained using the rule of law as one of the values that are also enshrined in section 3 of the Constitution or using the constitutional presumption that obliges right holders to consider the rights and obligations that are imposed by the constitution. The rule of law argument for instance enables regulators, law enforcement agents such as the Zimbabwe Republic Police (ZRP), border control teams and national courts to consider the regulatory framework when dealing with smugglers, dealers or consumers of *bronco*. The rule of law in this sense is simply used as governance according to a nation's laws or the higher law that is the constitution. In this case, the Zimbabwean society must simply appreciate the fact that there is no law that allows *bronco* to be licensed in Zimbabwe, notwithstanding that it is manufactured and could be legally used in South Africa. Those who smuggle it from South Africa or use it privately or sale it to the public must know that they can be arrested and prosecuted within the criminal courts of Zimbabwe without claiming any protection from the Constitution.

Using the normative theory, stakeholders must appreciate that the argument on *bronco* cannot strongly hold when dealing with growers and users of other drugs such as marijuana. Users of marijuana usually raise arguments that include traditional, religious, or medicinal purposes. The use of the normative theory in such instances helps legal reformers to either repeal the Dangerous Drugs Act (Chapter 15:02) or align it with the Constitution in light of the 'values' of the diverse people in Zimbabwe who believe in phantoms (*zvidhoma/zvindofa/zvitukwani*), spooks (*zvipoko/madzimudzangara*), avenging spirits (*ngozi*), *mweya yerudzi* (familiar spirits) and so forth. The Dangerous Drugs Act simply deals with plants from which dangerous drugs are derived to include a reference to the plant "Indian hemp", "bhang", "camba", "dagga", "mbanje" or "intsangu". It also imposes restrictions on the importation and exportation of drugs from the above plants except under and in accordance with the terms of a licence issued by the Minister. It excludes beliefs in many Shona communities where marijuana serves the same purposes with plants such as *rufandichimuka* (resurrection grass) or *zumbani* (fever tea tree) which is richer in anti-oxidants and rooibos. Traditional beliefs cement societies and it is high time that legal reformers and organizations dealing with constitutional literacy must prioritize community beliefs when designing ways to deal with drug users.

Followers of the indigenous Shona religion who use marijuana must be involved in reforming laws in a way that promotes a win-win situation between policy framers and policy takers. Recently, the government of Zimbabwe legalized the growing of marijuana to those who can afford to pay prohibitive license fees to grow and sell fresh or dried cannabis (Dzirutwe and Bolton 2018). Before the promulgation of the new ministerial regulations on cannabis use, those found in possession of the drug could be imprisoned for periods exceeding 12 years. The regulations and the enabling Act, the Dangerous Drug Actreferred to above are still lagging behind in terms of promoting an integration approach to dealing with the drug problem in Zimbabwe. There was need for the Minister responsible to consider factors such as the fact that those who use cannabis for traditional purposes were supposed to be consulted so that various community norms were made known to regulators to license the use of the drug in traditional healing or in conventional medical fraternity. Most importantly, there was need for regulators to demonstrate the role of CSOs in capacitating or training Zimbabwean law enforcement agents and the greater public to start considering the relationship between the norms in the Constitution and freedom of religion or conscience as a pillar of human rights. Clearly, policy framers need to solicit divergent viewpoints from drug users and the general populace in light of a value-based and human rights framework that are envisaged under the Constitution.

The Constitution as the Grundnorm was considered important in this chapter because it relates to the following areas that may be important in the control of drugs and drug trafficking within Zimbabwe and beyond to do the following:

(1) *Cooperation between quasi-judiciary institutions and security institutions.* Pseudo-judicial institutions such as ZIMRA play an important role in ensuring that goods are properly declared by those who enter into Zimbabwe. Major borders include Chirundu One-Stop border post which Zimbabwe shares with Zambia, Nyamapanda border post (Mozambique), Plumtree border post (Botswana) and Beitbridge Border Post (South Africa). The security institutions such as the Zimbabwe Republic Police (ZRP) and border control teams must intensify campaigns on how they are instrumental in arresting traffickers.

(2) *Reform and alignment of the drug laws.* The Dangerous Drugs Act is an important piece of legislation which guides courts on how to deal with traffickers. It is however outdated in that it has not been aligned with the Constitution. Pending alignment, the prohibited drugs in terms of that law are still important in shaping the formulation and implementation of the country's policy balance. Even subsidiary laws relating to licensing of the growing of marijuana or regulations on the movement of marijuana do not consider the views on traditional usage of drugs. These issues need to be urgently looked even from the perspective of patenting traditional knowledge for the benefit of Zimbabwe's intellectual property regime.

(3) *The structure of the border control and management teams.* The consequences of poor border management affect the whole of the Southern Africa

Development Community (SADC): countries which share borders with Zimbabwe, and countries which are part of SADC as a sub-regional bloc. Zimbabwe's drug policy and legal reform must borrow from South Africa's approach. The South African immigration department warns travellers not to bring certain drugs including birth control contraceptives. There are rigorous screening exercises and dog searches. Zimbabwe must also do the same when dealing with drugs smuggled from South Africa such as *bronco*. In the process, there is a lot on which Zimbabwe can tap from South Africa in shaping her drug policy.

(4) *The normative framework at a global level.* This was established by Resolution 42/112 of 7 December 1987, when the General Assembly decided to observe 26 June as the International Day against Drug Abuse and Illicit Trafficking as an expression of its determination to strengthen action and cooperation to achieve the goal of an international society free of drug abuse. Resolutions are soft law sources that States can use to develop their domestic laws. The Zimbabwean media fraternity and courts must use the day to campaign against drugs in Zimbabwe.

At international level, the normative framework laid out by the United Nations must attract an intense interest and concern of a great variety of people in Zimbabwe. Although the legal framework, as informed by the Dangerous Drugs Act, has not been aligned with the Constitution of Zimbabwe, 2013, Zimbabwe can take a big leaf from the UN's normative framework. The ministerial regulations in Zimbabwe show that license for mbanje growers can be refused when information has been received from a "peace officer, a competent authority or the United Nations" that an applicant was involved in the diversion of a controlled substance or precursor to an illicit market or use" (ibid). The involvement of the UN is important but all the laws in Zimbabwe must reflect this position. The significance of UNODC in giving impetus to the normative framework on the drug problem is that it is actively involved in the continuous monitoring and researching on global illicit *drug* markets in order to gain a more comprehensive understanding of their dynamics. What is clear from the above is this: a normative framework based more on the *'ought to be'* of law (as emphasized by utilitarian thinkers like Jeremy Bentham), than a positivist legal position which speaks to the '*what it is*' of the law (as emphasized by legal thinkers like John Austin, John Locke) is needed.

In the wake of the economic downturn and economic frustrations on the part of unemployed youths in urban Zimbabwe, or child-headed families in rural Zimbabwe, drug use may largely be explained from the need to minimize pain and maximize pleasure through the consumption of illicit brews. Alternatively, the youths can agree to be used as part of the chain of distribution of such drugs so that they earn a token fee. From such considerations, any serious and meaningful arguments on regulation, deregulation and re-regulation of illicit drugs such as *bronco*, *musombodhiya* (from ethanol) or any other pills or material such as glue must start from having a cultural-centered policy. Consequently, this chapter was dedicated to highlighting the dangers that are posed by the pockets of drug syndicates as well as the unreliability of weak partnerships between policy formulators and takers. The chapter also considers some of the motivating factors that prevent the generality of Zimbabwean citizens from becoming enthused with drug-related policy. Drug abuse becomes the case of the law hanging fruit for many sections of the society.

The proposition in this chapter

The proposition in this chapter was that if Zimbabwe is to have an effective policy on illicit drugs, then there is need to place emphasis on the fact that it is difficult to build consensus on beliefs in a diverse society. The chapter did not expect that all Zimbabweans would be amenable to respecting laws that ignore their sentiments on important aspects that affect their lives. While some of the citizens mainly flatly disagree with certain laws, others may welcome the laws especially on religious grounds. As such, the policy framers and legal reformers should keep close to the opinions of the public and use them to craft policies that bear on the values that unite the whole of the Zimbabwean society.

Why effective border control mechanisms?

The viewpoint in this chapter was considered justifiable simply because Westphalian nature of States focuses on State sovereignty using the philosophy of political realism. But realism which sees politics as a continuous struggle for power amongst nations is gradually being threatened by the actions of non-state actors and values from internationalism. While border security is important in ensuring that States determine their preparedness to deal with challenges posed by terrorists, transnational criminals and other illegal immigrants, or asylum seekers, poor border management causes States to lose a lot of revenue through corruption. As such, those who are eligible to enter into the country must be allowed to do so without event only if they comply with customs laws and regulation. In contradistinction, those who are ineligible must be deported or prohibited from entering the country. Those who are allowed to enter the country should also abide by the rules and regulations at the port of entry. Using the example from the United States (US), the need to emphasize on key external or national threats usually start at the border cannot be ignored. Rosenblum (2013) states that:

Understanding border risks begins with identifying key threats. At their roots, border-related threats are closely linked to the flow of people (travelers) and goods (cargo) from one country to another. Any smuggled item or individual hidden among the legitimate flows potentially constitutes a threat to U.S. security or interests. The intentions and actions of unauthorized travelers separate them into different threat categories, including terrorists, transnational criminals, and other illegal migrants. Illegal goods are distinguished by their inherent legitimacy or illegitimacy. Certain weapons, illegal drugs, and counterfeit goods are always illegal and categorically prohibited, while other goods are legal under most circumstances, but become illegitimate if they are smuggled to avoid enforcement of specific laws, taxes, or regulations.

Such an approach referred to above is not only important to the US, but to every nation that is serious in its fight on drug trafficking and transnational criminality. This is because the importance of categorizing travelers finds support from writings on the emergence of violent non-State actors. In their book entitled '*Drug Trafficking, Violence and Instability*', Williams and Felbab-Brown (2012) aptly captured the role that violent non-state actors (VNSAs) are playing in the drug game. Their book shows that the VNSAs are part of cartels or syndicates and serve as part of organized organizations. The rules of the drug game are getting complex and include avoiding designated borders (*thereby flouting immigration laws*), crackdown routes, and law enforcement officials. Clearly, and in all fairness, this chapter argued that State security or border control needs to take cognizance of various factors, including the increasing role of non-State actors. Williams and Felbab-Brown (ibid) also note that:

Violent challengers to the Westphalian state have taken different forms in different parts of the world. These forms include tribal and ethnic groups, warlords, drug trafficking organizations, youth gangs, terrorists, militias, insurgents, and transnational criminal organizations. In many cases, these groups are overtly challenging the State; in others they are cooperating and colluding with State structures while subtly undermining them; in yet others, the State is a passive bystander while violent armed groups are fighting one another. The mix is different, the combinations vary, and the perpetrators of violence have different motives, methods, and targets. In spite of their divergent forms, however, non-State violent actors share certain viii qualities and characteristics.

Against the background above, borders allow traffickers to establish transnational synergies which usually see the traffickers using borders or airports to smuggle illicit drugs. UNODC (2017) notes that the issue of cross-border criminal activities, such as trafficking in drugs, persons, firearms and cigarettes, terrorism and money-laundering is often linked to persons or organizations located well beyond the African continent. Zimbabwe must also seriously consider the need to comprehensively determine the extent to which smugglers work in cahoots with drug lords from other continents.

Why there is need for a thorough approach to drug trafficking?

Zimbabwe, as a significant actor in the global community needs to focus on the four pillars of the UNODC definition referred to above. Its researchers and institutions involved in areas that grow marijuana must be made available so that scholars and CSOs can easily prepare partnership documents which place emphasis on the urgency in reforming legislative policies that focus on cultivation, manufacturing, distribution and sale of illicit drugs. The type of the crop that is legally prohibited will also be known to the general public. Areas where illicit brews are manufactured, such as rural villages, and backstreets and street corners in urban areas have to be identified and effective measures taken to address the challenges posed by such activities. This move is informed by the fact that there is an abundance of literature on drug trafficking or its related challenges on most countries. It is no understatement to note at this juncture that nations the world over are affected differently and traffickers pose different problems to different countries. While The United Nations World Drug Report (2011) as cited in Dell (2012) for instance describes Mexico as '*the largest supplier to the U.S. illicit drug market, with Mexican drug traffickers earning approximately 25 billion USD each year in wholesale U.S. drug markets*', there are no such detailed comparisons that have been made to explain the relationship between Zimbabwe and its supplier countries.

Further, Guerrero (2011) as cited in Dell (ibid) states that:

> In addition to drugs, Mexican trafficking organizations engage in a wide variety of illicit activities including protection rackets, kidnapping, human smuggling, prostitution, oil and fuel theft, money laundering, weapons trafficking, arson, and auto theft

Unlike Zimbabwe where consumers usually harm themselves by drinking prohibited drugs such as *bronco*, some countries have deadly drug wars. With nearly 23000 intentional homicides in 2016 alone, Mexico's murder tally was only second to war-torn Syria's 60000 (Woody, 2017). Iran had roughly 17000 and Afghanistan 16000 (ibid). Such statistical information explains why Zimbabwe must take preventative measures before the drug problem escalates into unprecedented lethal levels.

Zimbabwe as a transit zone for illicit drugs

That the drug problem is explained in economic terms is beyond doubt. Drug traffickers have been described as economic actors with clear profit maximization motives (Dell, 2012: 1). In 2013, the Zimbabwe Revenue Authority (ZIMRA) commissioned a state-of-the-art non-intrusive scanner at the Chirundu One Stop Border Post (OSBP). The OSBP separates Zimbabwe from Zambia. Apart from showing that

ZIMRA is taking a lead in modernizing revenue collection methods, the former Commissioner General of ZIMRA, Mr. Pasi was quoted as having said that the use of the scanners would go a long way in facilitating the movement of containerized and other bulk cargo through the border post, by increasing the number of consignments that receive Customs attention without causing undue delay (ZIMRA, 2014). The scanners, with the capacity to scan 20 trucks per hour – would also help in *curbing illicit trade and drug trafficking* as well as improving the working environment for both the clients and staff (ibid) (underlining is intentionally made).

Curtis (2016), showed that trucks that pass through the OSBP include those from Zambia, South Africa, Namibia, and the Democratic Republic of Congo. The major consideration by Curtis (ibid) was the need to address the causes and magnitude of the long transit times that are experienced at the OSBP. This chapter argues that the length of the delays, reasons for the delays and recommendations that were proffered bear a lot of significance on Zimbabwe's preparedness to curb drug trafficking through Zimbabwe to countries such as Namibia, South Africa, DRC, or Zambia. In relation to the length of the delays for instance, Curtis (2009: xiii-xiv) states that:

On average, it took 39 hours for a truck to transit the Northbound through Chirundu and 14 hours the Southbound. This compared with 34 hours and 11 hours respectively for Beitbridge. Based on the Road Freight Association (RFA) estimates of the standing cost for a secondhand truck and flat deck semi-trailer, this equates to approximately US$31 million per annum. It means that the total cost of trucks standing at both Beitbridge and Chirundu is over US$60 million per annum. Add to this the cost of standing at other borders on the North-South corridor (Groblersbrug/Martins Drift, Kazungula, Nyamapanda, Zobue/Mwanza, Kasumbalesa) and the figure must be over US$100 million per annum and therefore transport prices along the corridor are inflated due to these delays.

The delays referred to above also add to other transit challenges that can emanate from the Nyamapanda and Beitbridge border posts. Although most of the challenges at the Chirundu border post were addressed by the introduction of the OSBP, the previous challenges can inform the tax collector on how to prevent leakages at other borders such as Nyamapanda where dangerous drugs like cannabis have been transported from Mozambique into Zimbabwe and South Africa. Zivira (2016) states that drug are smuggled from Mozambique and the truckers use refrigerated trucks. Before the introduction of the OSBP, it has been shown that refrigerated trucks were cleared quickly and the potential that several drugs were trafficked is very high. Curtis (2009) states that:

Refrigerated trucks and tankers are generally processed faster than break-bulk, consolidated or container traffic. Average transit times for these categories are 28 or 29 hours northbound compared to other categories that average 40 hours and upwards. However this needs to be brought down considerably and in line with Beitbridge where these loads transit in less than 10 hours

The above concern was made in relation to a regulatory decision to treat perishables with urgency. However, it is even more pertinent for ZIMRA to revisit its policies at all borders if credence is given to the observations by Zivira (ibid). The decision to physically search refrigerated trucks should be done efficiently. Reasonable steps can be taken to ensure that the truckers do not capitalize on administrative efficiency to transport illicit drugs.

Zimbabwe as a destination for illicit drugs

Amidst rampant border leakages, it is difficult for authorities to control the hemorrhaging in illicit drugs to and from Zimbabwe. Mataire (2016) rhetorically argues whether Mozambique has become a haven for drug trafficking. Several people have been arrested at the Nyamapanda border post. Instances of arrest include the arrest of a man who had 21 bags of cannabis, arrest of a Zimbabwean man who is employed by a South African company who was found in possession of 600kgs of cannabis.

Such illicit drug flows can never end unless security glitches are plugged by both Mozambique and Zimbabwean security agents as well as immigration officials. Mataire (ibid) states that Mozambican officials confirm that there are security leakages that cause contraband to enter into Zimbabwe through illegal check points. Mozambique has struggled to curb illicit flows since the 1990s because of the civil war. This again takes the argument into the need to examine the role of sub-regional blocs such as SADC in ensuring that there is political stability within the region. Added to this is the need for SADC States to understand the link between drug networks in Mozambique and Zimbabwe. Mataire (ibid) cites the United States Bureau of Diplomatic Security which indicated that there are probably two dominant networks: one led by Colombian drug lords and transports cocaine and the other one led by Pakistanis and Mozambicans who sell hashish and mandrax.

An effective method of reducing the inflow of illicit drugs on Zimbabwe is thus deduced from the concerns above and this includes:

- Acknowledging the role that is played by Zimbabwean citizens (including oversight institutions) in the trafficking of drugs from Mozambique into Zimbabwe and South Africa. For instance, the Zimbabwean trucker could have easily used his citizenship to fool officials at the Nyamapanda border post into Zimbabwe, or the Beitbridge officials to smuggle marijuana into South Africa had it not been for lady luck which did not smile at him.

- The need for security institutions explained in section 208 of the Constitution: the police, defence, intelligence, and Prison and correctional services to work closely with the Mozambican security officials in upping border patrols. This is particularly so considering that the driver of the truck that was impounded managed to escape without event.

- There is also need to accept that Mozambique serves as a transit zone for illicit drugs from other continents. Those drugs can end up in Zimbabwe. Zivira (2016) argues that such dangerous drugs usually find their way to Zimbabwe's capital city, Harare and that the young population in Harare's suburbs is usually affected. A country specific study has to be made out of a realization that families are being broken, the social fabric is being torn, food outlets and dancehall circles are becoming rendezvous for crime, and trafficking hotspots. Media practitioners such as Zivira have also provided researchers with insight on why Zimbabwe needs to have a practical goal: to develop and test control strategies that would be useful in the context of factors that explain the drug problem in Zimbabwe. The media investigation by Zivira (ibid) has not resulted in concrete guidelines for monitoring the drug problem since there was no verification of the role that is played by 'named' ministers and the police in encouraging complicit in drug trafficking.

- The logical corollary to the above questions can be put this way: *Who is involved in the trafficking of illicit drugs?* Lawn (1990) provides us with some vital information. He considers dispensers, distributors and manufacturers of controlled substances to include pharmacies, practitioners, hospitals, clinics, and teaching institutions. This brings to the fore the need for activists, researchers and regulatory authorities in Zimbabwe to investigate the major prescription drug problems that exist in the country. Lawn (ibid) states that prescription drugs have been identified in more drug-related deaths and emergency medical situations than all illegal drugs combined. Statistically, it has been shown that over twenty million Americans use prescription drugs for nonmedical reasons and that this problem stems from the misuse of prescription drugs and the diversion of controlled substances to the illicit market.

Further, what is currently obtaining in Zimbabwe is no different from how traffickers behave in the international community. For instance, Zivira (ibid) has shown that the syndicates are violent and include gangs that are powerfully working with runners in poor suburbs of Zimbabwe. They capitalize on the economic downturn to tear into citizens who are economically frustrated. This augurs well with the global concern that after decades of failing to adequately control drug consumption, an even graver problem has emerged: violent drug traffickers have taken the industry hostage and will stop at nothing to preserve their power (Jenner, 2011). For instance, while Zivira (2016) argues that Zimbabweans may be at risk for consuming drugs whose alcohol content may be over 95%, some of which are sold between $6 to $8 for 30 tablets, the United Nations Office on Drugs and Crime (UNODC), (2010) as cited in Bagley (2012) has also shown that although there is no definitive estimate, the value of all illicit drugs sold annually in the United States may reach as high as $150 billion.

UNODC as cited in Bagley (ibid) also notes that some $37 billion per year may be spent on cocaine alone. The debilitating effects of cocaine on the American society also justify why this current study is about the impact of dangerous drugs used in Zimbabwe that also include cocaine, marijuana, and chlorpromazine. The latter has been described as having an antipsychotic effect on the consumer. This then calls for an inter-ministerial approach to solving the drug problem in Zimbabwe.

Chapter Seven | Sharon Hofisi

The Ministry of Home Affairs for instance, can work together with the Ministry of Justice and Ministry of Health in having a baseline survey on the impacts of illicit drugs on Zimbabwe. This will go a long way in combating drugs and in changing attitudes of the syndicates, users, policy makers and the policy takers who include the generality of the population.

The spreading effects of drug trafficking have also been analyzed by scholars. International scholars have attempted to study the drug problem using various ways of encouraging States to find easy methods to deal with their own country-specific problems. Below are some of the ways in which scholars have described the approaches.

- *Treating drug trafficking as part of organized crimes in a country.* Bagley (2012: 1) has demonstrated that a country might best approach the problem through a detailed and critical review of the crimes that are linked to drug trafficking. He identified eight (8) aspects key trends or patterns that typify the on-going transformation of the drug trade and the organized criminal groups it has spawned as of mid-2011. They are: 1) The increasing globalization of drug consumption; 2) The limited or *"partial victories"* and unintended consequences of the U.S.-led '*war on drugs,*' especially in the Andes; 3) The proliferation of areas of drug cultivation and of drug smuggling routes throughout the hemisphere (so-called *"balloon effects"*); 4) The dispersion and fragmentation of organized criminal groups or networks within countries and across sub-regions (*"cockroach effects"*); 5) The failure of political reform and state-building efforts (*deinstitutionalization effects*); 6) The inadequacies or failures of U.S. domestic drug and crime control policies (*demand control failures*); 7) The ineffectiveness of regional and international drug control policies (*regulatory failures*); and 8) The growth in support for harm reduction, decriminalization, and legalization policy alternatives (*legalization debate*).
- *Moving towards universal jurisdiction.* Jenner (2011) moved for universal legalization of drug trafficking. This is very important and links to Bagley's seventh and eighth pillars. This is considered so in that law is simply defined as a set of rules and regulations affecting a society. The approach contemplated by Jenner (ibid) and Bagley (ibid) can inform Zimbabwe and countries such as Malawi, Lesotho,

Mozambique and South Africa to craft extradition laws that fit into the universal legalization model proposed above. Lesotho legalized the growing of marijuana and can work with countries which are normally affected by Zimbabwe's border control systems such as Malawi, Mozambique, Zambia and South Africa. Of course caution must be exercised if regard is had to the argument that the legalization theory is flawed because it rests on the assumption that drug laws, not drugs themselves, cause the most damage to society (Kerr, 1990).

- *The role of media monitoring and media reports.* Media reports on drug traffickers and the role of the police provide researchers with credible information on the role of the police and ministers. For instance, Razemba (2016) reported that 5 Zimbabweans were nabbed over $2.6m South Africa's drug haul. The South African police published the arrest on its website and also provided information that could be used by media houses to sensitize the general public that may not be able to access the internet. In the report by Razemba (ibid) showed that the 5 Zimbabweans were part of 8 suspects who were found in possession of 26kgs of heroin powder and 14kgs of uncut heroin with an estimated street value of R17 million. The economic effects of drug trafficking can then be weighed by treating the drug problem as part of an economic problem in a country. Zimbabweans can also utilize social media to campaign against drugs as has been the case with the use of social media to fight the stigma around HIV/AIDS and to campaign for political governance.

- *Development of sub-regional drug policies.* SADC and beyond are also examined since drug trafficking threatens national security and sub-regional integration. The chapter contended that unless academics and national researchers decide on the above questions, they cannot execute a good analysis on the controversies. If war on drugs is a war without strategy, that is one thing. If it is a global war, steeped in behavior change and transformative models that is quite a milestone. The chapter sets forth international normative principles that inform States and other stakeholders in the fight against drug trafficking. The author argued that Zimbabwe has an excellent legal infrastructure, in form of the Dangerous Drugs Act. The law has been utilized in deterring the general populace from dealing in dangerous drugs such as marijuana. However, there are challenges that relate to the implementation of the normative frameworks under the Constitution and international human rights law. Such principles have not been used to inform the drug policies and develop the laws within Zimbabwe and beyond its borders.

Why a furor on drug trafficking?

The rules of the drug game are also opaque and the players get to observe them under the fear of Machiavellian gangsters who operate in syndicates that start from the powers that be to the poverty-stricken rural or drain-warming urban youths who serve as the runners or distributors of illicit drugs. The information that is available is scanty and usually not verified officially. It is also limited to what is gathered by media experts, who for reasons that include media ethics cannot reveal the true identity of the users. Those allegedly identified as drug traffickers who end up getting arrested also suffer in the same way as the whistle blowers or informants in corruption cases can be victimized or even killed. Accused persons may usually be arbitrarily deprived of their constitutional freedoms such as the right to liberty because they do not know the informant's identity unless a court application is successfully made to have the identity revealed. This again brings to question the concern that legal models of combating illicit drugs are flawed because the laws do not start from the alleged trafficker.

It is argued in this chapter that normal, perceived or real problems of a phenomenon are effectively assessed by concentrating its demerits. In terms of illicit drugs and drug trafficking, it may be important to consider why drug abuse is rampant notwithstanding that drug laws provide useful insights on why complicit in drugs abounds amidst the existence of a regulatory framework. Simple questions such as '*What is an illicit drug?*' or '*what is drug trafficking?*' show how drug laws have caused the drug problem to be seemingly endemic the world over. An apt observation by scholars and researchers on how the American society is accustomed to quick fixes for its problems provide a clear caveat on how drug responses are not part of the quick solutions. Lawn (1990) states that those of us who are concerned with both drug supply and drug demand reduction have long recognized that there are no quick solutions. To him, the drug problem has been developing for a *long time, and it will take a significant amount of time to correct. Americans must allow recent drug abuse prevention and education programs to take root (italicizing is intentionally made).*

Although the argument by Lawn (ibid) was fed by the experience of a scholar who studied the drug problem in a more developed economy, the argument provides vital lessons for less developed countries like Zimbabwe which are also considered as sources and transit zones and destination for illicit drugs. Using the approach taken by Lawn (ibid), this study argues that a holistic approach is needed to explain for instance, why medicinal drugs are increasingly being used for non-medicinal purposes. Such an understanding needs active partnerships that seek to address the drug problem in a way that encourages the stakeholders to come ip with country-specific solutions. For instance, in their newspaper article on why there is abuse of prescription drugs in Zimbabwe, Chipunza and Razemba (2017) state that cross border traders are smuggling illicit drugs using haulage trucks or unscrupulous bus operators, mainly through Beitbridge border post. The drugs are offloaded at various premises and service stations in Simon Mazorodze (ibid). They are then transported to various centres such as Copacabana (bus terminus) in the central business district and high density suburbs such as Mabvuku, Kambuzuma, Mbare, Glenview, Mufakose and others (ibid).

The concerns raised by Chipunza and Razemba (ibid) dovetail with the findings by Zivira (2016). Zivira (ibid) states that the drugs that are commonly trafficked include broncleer (*bronco*), marijuana, chlorpromazine, diluted ethanol (ibid). Those drugs are ferried by truckers from Mozambique and Malawi into Zimbabwe. They are also ferried by bus drivers to countries like South Africa (ibid). They are usually smuggled through smaller border posts such as Chidodo in Muzarabani or larger posts such as Nyamapanda. The truckers connive with syndicates and put a layer of mbanje (marijuana) in their trucks before loading their normal shipment, which will then conceal the drugs (ibid). The illicit drugs are sometimes put in refrigerated trucks which are not subjected to physical searches at the borders because the truckers are assumed to be carrying perishables.

In identifying the players in drug trafficking, the two articles above showed that the following people have to be included in the drug equation:

- Cross border traders
- Truck and bus drivers
- Immigration officials
- Fleet owners
- Informal traders in the city centre
- Rank marshals and bus crew drivers
- Garage owners and fuel attendants
- Harare residents from Eastern suburbs such as Mabvuku, and western suburbs such as Glen View, Mufakose and Kambuzuma.

It also becomes clear that policies relating to the transportation of goods have to be reviewed periodically. Immigration officials must occasionally subject refrigerated trucks to search to inculcate a sense of responsibility in truckers. Similarly, the border control team must work with the members of the general public, especially through CSOs to convince the populace on why they may subject buses to search at places such as Simon Mazorodze near Harare. It is clear that Harare is several miles away from the Beitbridge border and members of the public may feel shortchanged if they are stopped near their drop off points. Regular campaigns and sensitization programs can give the border control team a buy-in from travelers who would understand that drug problem has far-reaching consequences. Literature shows that the search for sustainable solutions to drug trafficking in Zimbabwe, or at the least, an effective policy, has been at the very core of activists and researchers.

For Zimbabwe, the drug syndicates have been considered powerful, and though not verified, include politicians and ministers (Zivira, 2016). Two insights quickly become noticeable. Firstly, the minister and law enforcement agents, to the extent that they are involved, demonstrate the relationship between law and policy. Further, Ministers are failing to participate in the formulation and implementation of 'good' policies on drugs. This policy includes ensuring that border leakages are controlled. Zivira (ibid) describes the syndicates to involve truckers, politicians, the police and gangs who smuggle marijuana for instance from Mozambique and Malawi. Secondly, policy may end up influencing how drug laws are enforced by the law enforcement agents. Yet, the other syndicates who are supposed to be part of the policy takers have been seen to work with unemployed youths, who act as front men selling marijuana, cocaine and broncleer among other drugs (ibid). For Zimbabwe, most people are aware of the existence of a basic domestic structure of laws on dangerous drugs, but use drugs for reasons that are medically, traditionally, religiously and personally explained.

Lessons from what is obtaining across the globe

On 8 October 2009, the United Nations General Assembly (UNGA) held a meeting where the Third Committee was told that a successful fight against drug trafficking and transnational organized crime requires interlocking national, regional, international strategies. Quick notes on issues that came up as important in the fight against drug trafficking include:

- Eradicating the crops that are used to manufacture drugs
- Embarking on building counternarcotic infrastructure
- Emphasizing on alternative development programs as pillar to curb drug production
- Encouraging countries to appreciate and regularly visit the webpage of the United Nations Office on Drugs and Crime (UNODC) to get updated statistics on dangerous drugs like heroin and cocaine.
- Acceptance of the fact that African countries are being used as warehousing sites as well as transit routes for illicit drugs and precursor chemicals.
- Encouraging African states to appreciate growing trends cross-border criminal activities caused by porous borders, rogue States, weak immigration laws, financial technology, and intricate and accessible global transportation infrastructure which is dominated by non-State actors. West Africa has been hit hard by non-State actors who threaten national and regional security. In recent years, Nigeria has been affected by the actions of the Islamic State for West African Province (ISWAP), formerly or popularly known as Boko Haram. By declaring its allegiance to the Islamic State, ISWAP shows that it also moves towards the direction of establishing a caliphate in its areas of territorial dominance.

- The need to take a leaf from sub-regional groupings such as the Economic Community of West African States (ECOWAS), intergovernmental organizations involved in crime control such as Intergovernmental Action Group against Money Laundering in West Africa (GIABA) and regional rehabilitation organizations such as the African Institute for the Prevention of Crime and Treatment of Offenders.

Zimbabwe can benefit from the attendance of representatives from Zambia, the Holy See and International Organization for Migration (IOM) through inviting such attendees to participate in policy formulation on drugs. Bilateral trade and investment agreements with Zambia can also be designed with a bias towards combating drug trafficking and other organized crimes. The importance for working with Zambia is simply based on the fact that Zimbabwe shares the OSBP and both countries have been criticized for causing long transit times which may fuel drug trafficking. Moreover, the IOM has an office in Zimbabwe and strategic partnerships may be built in this regard.

What regulators and local drug users must urgently consider?

Regulators can only come into the picture if the players involved in the trafficking of illicit drugs are identified. Firstly, the definitional aspects of drug trafficking show that it is largely trade related. The countries of the world are guilty of being involved in illicit drug trade. There are those who cultivate or have drug traffickers who cultivate prohibited drugs. When focus is made on the prohibition of marijuana in Zimbabwe, it becomes important to locate the problem as part of religion and human rights. In some Zimbabwean circles, belief abounds as to the use of cannabis use: religious beliefs such as working as a medium of communication with the deity and traditional practices such as scaring away spooks, and healing mental ailments. Those who are adherents of religions that have hemp or marijuana as part of their religious arsenal, and believe the prohibition of such drugs is unconstitutional, may have to institute test cases in light of the national laws which prohibit drugs.

Apart from the Constitution, Zimbabwe has a Dangerous Drugs Act, as is also the case with countries such as Jamaica and Mauritius. The Act prohibits the use or misuse of certain drugs, places restrictions on imports and exports of drugs such as prepared opium and Indian hemp.The Zimbabwean legal framework deals with the importation, exportation, production, possession, sale, distribution and use of dangerous drug and fits well into the UN framework alluded to above. The Global Drug Policy Observatory may be used to supplement the UN normative framework. It describes Zimbabwe as still *'witnessing an increase in problematic drug use among its domestic population along with the related public health issues that accompany certain types drug use'*.

The substances that are most commonly used in Zimbabwe include alcohol, cannabis, heroin, glue and cough mixtures such as histalix and broncleer (*Bronco*). The latter is drunk with the mouth agape, because believably, all the teeth will disappear immediately. Imagine the health effects! Cannabis (*mbanje*) remains the most popular illicit drug mainly because it is grown locally or smuggled in from neighboring countries like Malawi and Mozambique. In some societies along the Zambezi, mbanje is grown and consumed in large quantities as a way of life.

Zimbabwe is also a conduit for the trafficking of drugs on their way to other countries in the region such as South Africa. Local Zimbabweans are often used to transport these drugs and rather than being paid in cash, they are usually paid in drugs which then enter the local market. "When you become a transit country, you are immediately also a consumption country.

Way Forward

- To reduce the drug problem, Zimbabwe needs to adopt the normative framework espoused by the UNODC and the Political Declaration and Plan of Action by the Commission on Narcotic Drugs. This would enable her to benefit from response mechanisms that have been adopted in some LDCs and MDCs as a way of curbing drugs.
- Zimbabwe also needs to learn from study approaches in countries that struggle to deal with trafficking problems. Dell (2012) for instance came up with a three pillar approach to studying the drug problem in Mexico. She found that the traffickers used (i) a network model of trafficking routes, (ii) plausible exogenous variation in local drug policy, and (iii) confidential data on the drug trade. In (i)

traffickers would minimize the costs of transporting drugs from producing municipalities to US entry points. They would take shortest routes that avoid municipalities that were involved in crackdowns. This may be used to avoid porosity in border post lie Chidodo which has been found to be the drug feeder post. In (ii) qualitative studies of events such as elections or violence have to be used to gauge the potential use of drugsin electoral violence or dancehall violence, since such areas have been identified as prone to drug trafficking and trade.

- Zimbabwe has to have an effective engagement strategy with countries that manufacture the drugs that are consumed in Zimbabwe or sold to South Africa. Zimbabwe is also supposed to craft drug polices that deal with drugs like 'musombodhiya, or nipa'. *Musombodhiya* is descriptive of street language that is used to refer to an illicit alcohol brew composed of diluted ethanol or methanol. The drug (because it contains high alcohol content) is alleged to contain 95 percent alcohol, is consumed in very small quantities and gives the consumer hours of drunkenness.

- Public awareness on the effects of drug abuse should be prioritized. Most beverages that are consumed in Zimbabwe have unknown alcohol content as shown above. This leaves unanswered questions as to whether or not the consumers are even aware of the impacts of alcohol on their health. Issues such as liver cirrhosis, passive smoking, and so on must be brought to the fore through public awareness campaigns. Apart from having no blood in their alcohol, the consumers often a time *"stick"* (*Kusitika*), which is the Zimbabwean way of describing a situation where the consumer is not able to move his or her body parts.

- There is need for effective institutional responses. Families, villages, provinces should be encouraged to work with the security institutions such as the Zimbabwe Republic Police (ZRP) in curbing the smuggling of ethanol. Most communities brew *Musombodhiya* to generate income for school fees and bringing food on the family table. They find it difficult to abandon a seemingly lucrative trade. *Musombodhiya* comes from ethanol which is reportedly smuggled from ethanol plants and is then diluted with water, sold for about US$1 for the 100ml or US$7 for the 750ml bottle. An institutional approach is important because organizations have different strategies of promoting a buy-in from the community. While the ZRP for instance has to devise a drug control model; the community has to help cultivate a sense of responsible citizenry and CSOs assist in reforming drug survivors. The end result, however, is that the three institutions unite in having a strong emphasis upon the need to curb the use of drugs.

- There is also need to document the various types of alcoholic beverages that are produced in Zimbabwe for sale in Zimbabwe or to neighbouring countries. The areas where illicit substances such as *musobhodhiya, kachasu (nipa), chikwakubidiri* (one day brewed beer) are brewed have to be known. Civil society organizations must work with such areas to avoid chances of drug-related problems. The Government must also ensure that self-help projects are supported since the producers usually use poverty as a motivating factor.

- Because a radical focus on the drug laws has been seen as flawed, there must be a radical shift in designing sentencing policies to guide magistrates in our criminal courts. The sentence must also take cognizance of international trends. It must not end on retributive punishment. Those guidelines must give due regard to the Constitution, particularly religious freedom.

- The Dangerous Drugs Act and the Criminal Law (Codification and Reform) Act must also be urgently aligned with the Constitution. While the laws contain certainly good sentencing guidelines, there is no indication of the approaches to constitutional freedoms.

- There is also need to embrace the objectives of UNODC Southern Africa which include

o Strengthening the legislative and judiciary capacity of Southern African countries to ratify and implement international conventions and instruments on drug control, organized crime, corruption, terrorism and money laundering

o Assisting such countries in reducing drug trafficking and in controlling precursor chemicals

o Enhancing the capacity of Government institutions and civil society organizations in SADC to prevent drug use and the spread of related infections, including HIV/AIDS, among youth and other vulnerable populations, particularly in prison settings.

o Enhancing the capacity of Government institutions and civil society organizations in the Southern African region to counter trafficking in persons and smuggling of migrants

o Creating awareness about and reducing the incidence of domestic violence in Southern Africa in cooperation with civil society and Governments

o Promoting victim empowerment by improving coordination, building capacity and strengthening relations between Governments and civil society in order to improve services to victims, especially women and children.

Conclusion

From the foregoing indications on the problematic nature of drugs, Zimbabwe has made some strides through impounding trucks in transit and establishing an OSBP. However, there is urgent need for Zimbabwe to move towards an integrated approach to the regulation of the distribution and sale of drugs. This approach must involve the ordinary citizen, health regulatory bodies, Pharmacies, and Ministries such as Home Affairs, Health and Justice, Information. The starting point must be the drugs themselves, then the drug laws. The current approach focuses on legal violations but does not consider the reasons why Zimbabweans use certain drugs. More to this point is the endeavor of those citizens who are willing to share their lived realities on social platforms on how they benefited from the CSOs, health institutions, or lenient sentences that were imposed on them by courts as well as the correctional approaches that they received when they were incarcerated.

The argumentation in this endeavor is that these approaches lead us to deal with the issues to drug trafficking in a holistic manner. Those who misuse or use dangerous drugs are also empowered to speak out without fear of being prosecuted. This in no way indicates the need to condone the use or misuse of illicit drugs. It is however much the same fallacy as to say the youths are the ones who consume the highest levels of drugs because they engage in high risk behaviour. The same obtains where one religious movement is identified as the leading consumer of drugs such as marijuana. There is no logical or legal basis for assertions of this kind when the only basis are court cases where those arrested and brought before the courts may be tried and convicted or acquitted of the crime of possessing dangerous drugs.

Further, an examination of some criminal cases will also show that there was no evidentiary sufficiency but many factors led to the conviction of the accused person. He could have been unrepresented, failed to proffer some exceptional circumstances relating to the possession or the plausibility of his defence was not properly weighed together with the evidence. The ZRP sometimes does not reveal the identity of the informant and this highly prejudices the accused persons in terms of preparing their defence. This works to the detriment of effective crime control. Added to this argument is the fact that those who brew illicit beer at their backyards or in street corners are usually spared the wrath of the law. The reasons for not arresting them range from corruption to organized criminality between the brewers and the consumers. Again the fact that their brews are *'unspoken'* does not mean that there was no illicit beer that was brewed. It simply points to the fact that the perpetrators were neither arrested nor prosecuted.

It takes, from the foregoing, something more than the definition of dangerous drugs or the identification of leakages at the borders to enable a nation to effectively deal with drug trafficking. The UN approaches must be promoted by the government and CSOs in the same way specific country experiences must be taken seriously for the benefit of all Zimbabweans. In other words, while there is a general legal framework on drugs in Zimbabwe, a theory of positive social change or a sound theory of rights and responsibilities must be adopted which promotes an integrated approach to solving drug-related issues. Such as theory must start to appreciate that legalization is no effective than knowing the drug. The theory must also inform the government to urgently align laundering laws, drug laws, immigration laws, and various criminal laws with the Constitution. Quientesentially, consequentialist theories of punishment such as rehabilitation and general deterrence of offenders must also be considered when dealing with drug dealers or consumers found to be in conflict with the law.

References

Bagley, B (2012) 'Drug Trafficking and Organized Crime in the Americas: Major Trends in the Twenty-first Century' Woodrow Wilson International Centre for Scholars.

Curtis, B. (2009) *'The Chirundu Border Post Detailed Monitoring of Transit Times'* Word Bank, available at http://siteresources.worldbank.org/E XTAFRSUBSAHTRA/Resources/DP10-Chirundu.pdf, accessed 14/08/2017.

Dell, M (2012) *'Trafficking Networks and the Mexican Drug War'* Harvard University Department of Economics.

Dzirutwe, M and Bolton, A (2018) 'Zimbabwe Says Will Issue Cannabis Licenses to Growers', Reuters.

Jenner, M.S (2011) 'International Drug Trafficking: A Global Problem with a Domestic Solution', Indiana University Maurer School of Law

Kerr, 'The Unspeakable is Debatable: Should Drugs Be legalized? New York Times.

Lawn C.J (1990) *'The Issue of Legalizing Illicit Drugs'* Hofstra Law Review

Mataire, L (2016) 'Has Mozambique become a Haven for Drug Trafficking?'The Southern Times

Ngomani, S (2016) 'A Botanical Treasure Called Mapfura' UNESCO.

Razemba, F. (2016) *'5 Zimbabweans Nabbed in $2.6m SA Drug Hall'* The Herald, available at http://www.herald.co.zw/5-zimbabweans-nabbed-in-26m-sa-drug-haul/accessed 13/8/17

Rosenblum M.R (2013) *'Border Security: Understanding Threats at U.S. Borders'* Congressional Research Services.

Tsakiwa, T (2012) 'Zimbabwe: Low-down on Drugs', Herald

UNODC (2017) *'Border Control'* UNODC, available at https://www.uno dc.org/westandcentralafrica/en/newrosenwebsite/TOC/border-control.html, accessed 15/08/17

Williams, P and Felbab-Brown (2012) *'Drug Trafficking, Violence, and Instability'* University of Pittsburgh.

Woody, C (2017) 'Mexico's Drug-War Death Tollin 2016 Reportedly Exceeded Murder Levels in Many Countries Mired in War' Reuters.

ZIMRA (2014) *'ZIMRA Commissions a Non-Intrusive Scanner'*, ZIMRA, available at http://www.zimra.co.zw/index.php?option=com_conte nt&view=article&id=2096:zimra-commissions-a-non-intrusive-

scanner&catid=4:story&Itemid=85, accessed 14/08/2017. Zivira, T, *'Zimbabwe: Inside Harare's Dark Illegal Drug Trafficking Syndicates'* The Standard, 29 February 2016, available at http://allafrica.com/sto ries/201603011035.html, accessed 13/08/1

Chapter Eight

Drug Trafficking and Border Management in Zimbabwe

Charles Mutasa

Introduction

Drug trafficking is a global illicit trade involving the cultivation, manufacture, distribution and sale of substances which are subject to drug prohibition laws. Global increases in problems of illicit drugs have led to many development-related tensions including ill-health, social unrest, reduced family and community cohesiveness, economic sabotage and increased crime (Jenner, 2011). For Zimbabwe, the emergency of new and deadly drugs (cough syrups and illicit alcohol beverages) being abused mostly by younger males in high density suburbs is worrying (Tsiko, 2017). The drug abuse has become a major cause for admissions into mental hospitals in the country.

Paradoxically, economic and technological developments while promoting economic growth also unwittingly provide opportunities for drug producers and traffickers to organize themselves in cartels to easily make profits by distributing illicit drugs in all parts of the world. For example, the producers of marijuana, heroin, coca leaf and cocaine in developing countries like Peru, Bolivia and Colombia, easily get them marketed in the United States, Canada, Great Britain, Western and Eastern Europe. It is unfortunate that global policies and instruments designed to control the supply of illicit drugs have not produced satisfactory results. In Zimbabwe, the Ministry of Health and Child Welfare estimates that 1, 3 million people suffer from mental disorders linked to substance abuse (Tsiko, 2017). This is happening at a time when there are no mental health facilities and dwindling support to care institutions.

The purpose of this chapter is to discuss drug trafficking and border controls in Zimbabwe. In so doing, it also discusses the social impact of drug abuse and consequences that drug trafficking have had on the Zimbabwean society- families, health, education, crime and employment. The chapter ends with recommending the need for more information and research on drug abuse. The government has to do more to tackle the problems of substance abuse. A number of recommendations suggesting how problems of drug abuse prevention and control can be addressed in a constructive and coordinated manner are given. The chapter begins with a global and regional overview of drug trafficking and border controls before focusing on the case of Zimbabwe.

International Context

The movement of drugs from their production sites in developing countries often involved the use of foreigners, who operate in cartels. The commonly spoken of routes include Malaysia, Thailand, Hong Kong and China. To avoid capture and seizure of their drugs, the cartels more often than not device new sophisticated ways of packaging and concealing their products from law enforcement agents, and thereby reducing the chances of interdiction at border control points. Women have become special agents in both production and distribution of drugs (Anderson, 2017). This reveals women's relative powerlessness to domineering males in illegal street-based drug markets. Given the political, social and economic woes in less-developed countries, poor men and women are often recruited to facilitate the illicit drug trafficking trade (Wright et al, 1993). Those caught by immigration or border officials are easily replaced as the business continues. Poverty often drives poor people to be couriers of drugs. For instance, Zimbabwean students in Cyprus are said to have been dragged into drug trafficking in order to pay for tuition fees and upkeep in foreign countries. There are revelations that a number of duped Zimbabwean students studying in Cyprus are being forced into crime and prostitution after being offered fake university scholarships in Harare (Paradza, 2017). Upon arrival in

Cyprus, they realize that the scholarships do not exist and they are forced into prostitution and drug trafficking as ways of helping themselves out of the predicament. Drug trade often generates enormous sums of money for those involved, but it also leads to other forms of organized crimes including armed robbery and armed dissident activities.

Sustainable Development Goals 3 and 16 are at the heart of the work of the United Nations Office for Drugs and Crimes (UNODC). The former – ensuring good health and well-being – sees the Office promoting an approach grounded in health, social protection and cohesion, and pays special attention to the people, groups and countries most in need. The latter – which looks to promote peace, justice and inclusive societies – is reflected in UNODC's work to provide normative, analytical and operational assistance to Member States to strengthen the effectiveness, fairness and accountability of their criminal justice institutions to tackle illicit drugs, among others(UNDOC, 2017). UNDOC's broad mandate includes tackling illicit drugs, promoting health and alternative mechanisms.

The United Nations reports trends in drug use and abuse from a variety of sources. However, it is worth noting that most sub-Saharan African countries do not systematically do reports on drug trafficking and abuse to the United Nations. Almost one third dare do their reporting to the United Nations, making it difficult to assess trends. Drug abuse in Africa, especially among women is said to be on the increase due to prevailing political, social and economic crisis. A decrease has been noted in the Islamic states of Iran, Qatar and Bahrain (UNDOC, 1995). This is probably due to stiffer penalties for drug abuse and strict adherence to Islamic laws.

People take drugs as a result of many factors: pain or stress relief, peer pressure, self-esteem and leisure. Drug abuse has put a heavy burden on communities in many countries, frequently overloading health and welfare, treatment and law enforcement agencies. Substance abuse weaken the sense of belonging to a group, place and people (Jurich et al, 1985). Drug use by peers may exert a greater influence than the attitudes of parents. Research has shown that peer and parental influences are synergistic, with the highest rates of marijuana use being observed among adolescents whose parents and friends were drug users (UNDOC, 1995). It is well known that having biological relatives with alcoholism increases the risk in unaffected individuals. The problems of male partners may affect women in the form of difficulties in interpersonal relationships, instability, violence, child abuse, economic insecurity, deprivation of schooling and risk of sexually transmitted disease, including HIV infection. Drug abuse is often associated with depression, anxiety and severe mental illness. Overall, drug abuse affects, individuals, families, institutions and society at large.

The Zimbabwean Context

Drug trafficking represents a major challenge for Zimbabwe, particularly its porous borders with Mozambique, South Africa, Zambia and Botswana that have turned it into a major transit country for illicit drugs. The HIV epidemic in the country affected primarily sex workers, people who inject drugs and men who have sex with men (MSM). Zimbabwe reportedly spends millions of dollars annually trying to control drug abuse. On 29 July 2016, the Government of Zimbabwe launched its Trafficking in Person National Plan of Action (hereafter "NAPLAC") and adopted the Blue Heart Campaign on the occasion of the commemoration of World Day Against Trafficking in Persons in the capital, Harare (UNDOC, 2016).

Abuse of prescription drugs and pills continues to be on the increase among youths as cross border traders, bus operators and unscrupulous truck drivers smuggle the substance into the country. Most drug consignments include mental health tablets known as the blue tablet or cough syrup such as "BronCleer" referred to as "Bronco" in street lingo (The Herald, 6 March 2017:5). Bronco is not licensed for sale in Zimbabwe. Some of the drugs abused in Zimbabwe include alcohol, tobacco, inhalants (solvents), mandrax, sedatives, tranquilisers, and cannabis. Drug abuse tends to increase with age and locations. Urban areas and schools seem to have more drug abuse problems than rural areas and other institutions. Psychoactive drugs such as cocaine, heroin, Benzodiazepines, zed, and diazepam-"musombodhiya" have an impact on thinking, mood and behaviour (The Chronicle, 20 April 2017:4).

The Ministry of Health as part of demonstrating its commitment to agreed global undertakings, often teams up with NGOs, and the private sector and other stakeholders, every 26th of June to commemorate the International Day Against Drug Abuse and Illicit Trafficking. Zimbabwe does not have drug rehabilitation centres and it uses psychiatric institutions to rehabilitate drug addicts. According to the Ministry of Health Manager, Ms. Eneti Siyama, 57% of all admissions to psychiatric institutions are due to drugs and alcohol abuse(The Herald, 6 March 2017:5). The areas worst affected by drug abuse is Harare, Bulawayo and some parts of Mashonaland. Drug abuse has resulted in many youth committing heinous crimes and suffering from microbial resistance caused by abuse of medication.

This chapter derives its information from literature review, interviews and focus group discussions held with various key informants. Chapter focus is mainly on drug use and trafficking, which has affected the livelihoods of most youths and defied border controls of many African countries

Drug Tracking at Zimbabwe Borders

With the current economic challenges and increasing social unrest, there are claims that many drug dealers from Asia, South America and Europe are finding Zimbabwe as a safe haven for dangerous drugs. The Canine Unit, which brings together the Zimbabwe Revenue Authority (Zimra) and security agents to fight border crimes including the smuggling of drugs, reported in its annual reports that it had 128 detections in 2017 compared to 115 in 2016. It further reported that contraband consisting of 7 062,5kgs of cannabis, 9kgs of cocaine and 10, 3 litres of injectable omnipaque drug was intercepted (Moyo, 2018). ZIMRA has been charged with the control of the import and export restrictions and prohibitions of hazardous substances, dangerous, harmful and expired drugs.

Zimbabwe currently does not have a drug policy but two pieces of legislations are used to control the manufacturing, dealings and distribution of drugs in Zimbabwe. Zimbabwe's Dangerous Drugs Act [Chapter 15:02] criminalizes trading in drugs by unauthorized individuals and companies. In the recent past, punishments for illegal trade were common for the following common drugs, among many others: cannabis (also known as "dagga"/"mbanje", coca leaves, coca bush, and

Opium (raw and prepared). The Criminal Law Codification Act is used to punish those found in unlawful possession, dealing, using, hiding, disguising or benefitting from the proceeds of dangerous drugs. A person can be sent to prison for 15 to 20 years for importing, exporting, selling, advertising, transporting, delivering, cultivating, producing, administering, possessing, supplying and procuring dangerous drugs without a permit. Zimbabwe is a signatory to international instruments dealing with issues of drug abuse and trafficking including the 1961 U.N. Single Convention on Narcotic Drugs, the 1971 U.N. Convention on Psychotropic Substances, the 1988 U.N. Convention against Illicit Traffic in Narcotic Drugs and Psychotropic Substances, and the SADC (Protocol on Combatting Illicit Drug Trafficking).

The threat to combating drug trafficking just like corruption is largely associated with its lucrative venture, which brings in high profile politicians and senior civil servants. Most drug dealers and trafficking syndicates are advanced and complex, highly capable of evading law enforcement agents or oiling their hands. Atega (1998) argues that most illicit drug traffickers go undetected at border posts. Goredema (2011) maintains that drug smugglers in Southern Africa including Zimbabwe appear to be versatile and successful in using their transportation and network systems to move drugs despite the existence of some border check points and detection methods.

A number of Zimbabweans have been caught in other countries trying to smuggle drugs. With economic difficulties facing the country, South Africa by virtue of being a neighbouring country has reported several illicit drug trafficking cases to/from Zimbabwe via the Beitbridge boarder post. The World Drug Report (WDR) 2010, noted that Zimbabweans constituted 1% of people from different nationalities who trafficked hard drugs into Pakistan, while Nigerians and Tanzanians constituted 32% and 4% respectively. Three Zimbabwean women were sentenced to death in China for trafficking cocaine and heroin (*The Africa Report. 2011*).

Civil Society working on Drug Issues

A number of civil society organizations (CSOs) work on strategies aimed at awareness raising and promotion of healthy and safe use of drugs, as well as rehabilitation of drug addicts. Some of these organizations are the Zimbabwe Civil Liberties and Drug Network (ZCLDN) and the Anti-Drug Abuse Association of Zimbabwe (ADAAZ). Government still needs to create a more conducive environment for joint work with most CSOs in the country.

ZCLDN is a non-profit organization, which advocates for effective strategies for addressing problems associated with drug use in Zimbabwe. Its major objective is to influence and contribute to the formation of drug policies that are responsive to public health and human rights. ZCLDN engages with government, media, civil society organizations on drug laws, and harm reduction strategies for drug users, influencing perceptions on drugs, public health and safe use of drugs within the country coupled with other public initiatives such as the fight against HIV and TB. Sofia Mapuranga, the ZCLDN Media Officer said, ".... [We emphasize] on the importance of ensuring that even those with drug addictions have their rights honoured, including the right to health care" (Mutingwende, 2016).

ADAAZ is an anti-drug abuse lobby group, which is into advocacy, research and documentation, providing statistics on use of drugs and substances as well as facilitating dialogues between citizens and policy makers. ADAAZ claims that many youths are turning to consumption of or trading in illegal drugs or substances as a way of drowning their sorrows and frustrations over their unemployment and economic distress. It also claims that about 43% of students in high school have used or come in contact with some illegal drugs or substances (Lawhub, 2017). ADAAZ notes that youths are into drugs due to a number of problems including family break downs, peer pressure, physical abuse, and high unemployment.

People Who Use Drugs (PWUD)

According to the Drug Abuse Association of Zimbabwe (ADAAZ), Zimbabwe has a growing drug use problem but there has not been a coordinated approach to addressing the extent of this problem. Drug users are a key population when it come to the global definition but this has not trickled down to the Zimbabwean context because there is no agreed definition of what a key population group is composed of according to one of the key informants at ADAAZ. There is no reliable data, statistics and the population size estimate of the extent of the problem and the clear linkages to HIV hence the support to this section and group unlike men having sex with men (MSM) and sex workers has not been substantial. Key informants highlighted that drug users are also susceptible to infections due to their substances use where they may share syringes when using injectable drugs (FGD, 2017). Drug use is very rampant among sex workers and is a common resort to coping with stigma and discrimination among lesbians, gay, bisexual, and transgender (LGBTIs). The Zimbabwe Civil Liberties Network (ZCLDN), according to its Director, Wilson Box has received limited support from individual politicians such as the late Dr Timothy Stamps. The organization enlisted the support of a member of parliament Hon. Monica Mutsvangwa to prepare a draft motion on Drug Policy Reform which was expected to be tabled in parliament in January 2018. The main challenge identified is that in the absence of a comprehensive Drug Use Policy even decision makers are not sure how to tackle the challenge and in some cases completely oblivious to extent of the challenge (ZCLDN, 2016).

Currently both ZCLDN and the National AIDS Council, have limited support for the cause of PWUD as they have not made a compelling case on the linkages between drug abuse and HIV and AIDS to elicit support of more partners. Decision makers and service providers such as hospitals, clinics and the police are still discriminatory towards PWUD in the absence of a drug policy that would have ensured complete treatment and medical support/rehabilitation for drug users in Zimbabwe. At present the laws of Zimbabwe criminalise drug users. Hence it is often reported that drug users are arrested when untrained health workers secretly call the law enforcers to apprehend drug users who have walked through to seek health services. On the other hand, churches have tried to assist drug users, however, they do not have the capacity or know-how relating to drug users or their rehabilitation. Most religious leaders often view drug use as being caused by demons and resort to attempting to exorcise such evil spirits. This process often involves exposing oneself before the church as a drug user and can lead to the community stigmatising a known drug user. According to drug users however, their biggest challenge is with the police and health workers who both stigmatize and ill-treat drug users as they are perceived as being a nuisance to society. Health workers do not prioritise them and in several cases, refer them for psychiatry support.

Drug users experience stigma and discrimination at different levels starting with the family, community, the local health facility and also when exploring employment opportunities. PWUDs are profiled as risky employees and this has reduced their opportunities to be gainfully employed. In this regard there is need for a drug policy reform to address the stigma and discrimination, the criminalisation of drug users and support equal access to health and economic opportunities(The Herald, 6 March 2017:5). Most drug users are aware that most health institutions do not prioritise them but view them as "outcasts" or mentally ill hence they are not willing to go to health facilities. The laws of Zimbabwe criminalise drug users as they are often arrested when seeking health services in a clinic or hospital. Treatment for drug users is also not easy. As drug users themselves expressed, self-stigmatization due to them being viewed as outcasts means they usually misinform health workers on their illness. Such information is also useful to ensure they are treated just like other patients. There is great need for the police and the judiciary to be trained on how to relate with drug users.

There are stereotypes, prevalent in communities that contribute to stigmatization of drug users. These mainly include the community wide perception that male drugs users are thieves and societal outcasts who do not need any form of assistance and the female drug users are all prostitutes. Such stereotypes also affect health workers and usually influence how they treat drug users regardless of what the user is going through. The health workers strongly stigmatize drug users dismissing them with statements like "Anonwa ngemba (also known as the blue pill or diazepam) uyo" (meaning he is under the influence of drugs for psychiatry patients) because they believe that it is not a sickness and that it is self-inflicted (FGD, 2017). Men and women who use drugs in relation to their health needs and priorities, face barriers to accessing health care and HIV prevention services. Women PWUDs experience sexual harassment and gender based violence from their partners or acquaintances who at times try to take advantage of their intoxication. When PWUDs report such cases of abuse this is not treated seriously or it's dismissed as not reliable due to the fact that they use drugs. Terms such as "Bitch Bronco" or "Fire Sister" are used to refer to those women who had become drug addicts particularly with 'BonCleer' flu medication as their drug of choice. These negative connotations on female drug users made it more challenging for female drug users to access treatment as the stigma is greater for female drug users. Female sellers of drugs usually also engaged in sex work hence creating another intersection of drugs and sexual activity.

Traditional leaders have been influencing the culture of stigmatization against drug users. They are yet to accept that it requires medical attention. The chiefs particularly need to be sensitized and capacitated on how to address issues of drug users. Drug users are aware that religious leaders also contribute to stigma and discrimination since in some cases they relate to drug users as being possessed by demons and in many cases they are in denial of the problem. Drugs users recommended that "religious leaders need to be trained on the how to relate with drug users." At community level there is need to sensitive various community structures and especially the family on the issues of drug users and to confront the stigma. Sensitization has to start at the family level because this is where stigma is most felt as well as the effects of drug use or abuse.

Another key aspect brought by drug users interviewed was the complicity of political leaders and the police in handling some cases since drug use is fuelled by the drug industry which is quite lucrative. Hence there are many places that openly sell drugs and are never shut down because they belong to someone prominent or someone who is in the police force. Certain drugs enter the country through the health sector, requiring licenses which can only be obtained from high level people hence it is difficult for political leaders to tackle drug use since this is where some of the leading sellers reside.

Chapter Eight | Charles Mutasa

Youths and drugs

Zimbabwe has a youthful population with over 60% of the people, being lower than 35years of age and the majority unemployed. The Anti-Drug Abuse Association of Zimbabwe reveal that there is a rise in drugs abuse among youths with an increasing proportion of drug abusers in schools. Drug abuse often result in a lowered commitment to education, declining grades, absenteeism from school, increased potential for dropping out, illnesses, accidents, suicide and homicide (Financial Gazette, January 29, 2015). A number of families become dysfunctional as most young adolescents and youths become dependent on parents and relatives for their welfare and fending for themselves. Youths who use drugs are often alienated and stigmatized by their peers.

Organizations such as Active Youth Zimbabwe (AYZ) have been assisting students with fighting drug abuse, especially alcoholism. After realizing the upsurge in drug abuse in schools, AYZ partnered with the Ministry of Primary and Secondary Education to educate teachers around Bulawayo on drugs and substance abuse. AYZ has been counselling and providing guidance to a number of students (AYZ, 2017). At national level, the Zimbabwe Republic Police (ZRP) Victim Friendly Units, the National AIDS Council, Childline and several NGOs are working on campaigns to educate teenagers on unsafe sex, drug and alcohol use. Key concerns around deviant social behaviour among youths is the increase in HIV infections. Through guidance lessons and using 'a catch them young approach, the AYZ acquired knowledge is passed on to students, who in many cases found in possession of dagga.

In both Harare and Bulawayo, growing youth illicit behaviour is linked to drug abuse is sex parties, commonly known as "vazum or pasa pasa's" (Gumbo, 2015). At these parties, young people engage in illicit behaviour such as drugs, alcohol and dangerous sexual activities.

Zimbabwe is to deploy drones to help in the fight against drug trafficking and smuggling, Deputy Minister of Home Affairs Obedingwa Mguni told the Senate (Rukuni, 2018). Teenager drug problems in Zimbabwe are related to the use of addictive substances such as glues, tobacco, alcohol and thinners. Deaths as a result of drug abuse still remain a major concern. The Ministry of Health and Child Care's Department of Mental Health indicated that 135 drug-induced psychosis admissions were recorded at Harare Hospital alone in 2013, with 865 outpatients documented in the same year (Financial Gazette, January 29, 2015).

Sex Workers and Drug Abuse

Sex workers find it necessary to take drugs in performing their duties as they found it abnormal to attend to many clients and also meet their demands in their sober minds (FGD, 2017). Sex workers in Bulawayo confirmed during an FGD that they find it necessary to take drugs in performing their duties as they found it abnormal to attend to many clients and also meet their demands in their sober minds. Drugs help them cope with client demands and in many cases clients offer them drugs before sexual encounters. This emphasises the need to develop a proper response to drug use because of the linkages to HIV transmission and ART adherence. Drug use can be a risk to HIV transmission and also inhibit ART adherence when the drugs are used excessively as part of a daily routine of different key population groups. This situation also points to the need for a gendered 'intersectional' response which recognises the fluidity and multiplicity of identities and behaviours within and between key populations groups. Although the sex workers narrated the use of drugs in their business, they were also quick to recommend the need for teachings regarding reduction of any form of harm and high risk that may be associated with drug abuse. Basically they underscored the need for holistic interventions that help them get more teachings on safe use of drugs, methods of empowering sex workers, prevention and care for HIV and sexually transmitted infections (STIs), the decriminalisation of sex workers, and a rights based approach prioritising the self-determination of sex workers. They claim that drugs help them cope with client demands and in many cases clients offer them drugs before sexual encounters. This emphasises the need to develop a proper response to drug use because of the linkages to HIV transmission and ART adherence.

Drug use can be a risk to HIV transmission and also inhibit antiretroviral therapy (ART) adherence when the drugs are used excessively as part of a daily routine of different key population groups

(National Aids Council, 2017). This situation also points to the need for a gendered 'intersectional' response which recognises the fluidity and multiplicity of identities and behaviours within and between key populations groups. Although the sex workers narrated the use of drugs in their business, they were also quick to recommend the need for teachings regarding reduction of any form of harm and high risk that may be associated with drug abuse. Basically they underscored the need for holistic interventions that help them get more teachings on safe use of drugs, methods of empowering sex workers, prevention and care for HIV and sexually transmitted infections (STIs), the decriminalisation of sex workers, and a rights based approach prioritising the self-determination of sex workers.

Salient issues worth considering

A number of issues stick out when dealing with issues of drug abuse and border controls in Zimbabwe. Some of the pertinent issues worth considering are the following:

- Zimbabwe had no drug policy masterplan at the moment. So there was need to address the issue.
- Those who abuse drugs seem to have the same access to the same drugs after rehabilitation, making the entire process of trying to resolve the problem a cycle of despair for service providers.
- There are no specialized facilities to treat drug abusers in Zimbabwe. Sadly drug injection is contributing to HIV/AIDs, hepatitis B and C and TB.
- The lack of effective advocacy and lobbying mechanisms for effective, workable appropriate science-based drug laws, policies and consistent with best international practices on the subject of drug use and misuse in a modern open democratic society which upholds the civil liberties of persons is a major cause for concern (Towo, 2018).

Conclusion

Overall, on one hand, there is need to decriminalize drug use and support users through public health initiatives. On the other hand it seems border controls are easily managed if illicit drugs deals are minimized or brought to a halt. The government of Zimbabwe needs to introduce harm reduction strategies and drug policy reforms that make it easy for drug addicts/users to feel welcomed within health institutions and society at large. Adopting a human rights approach to resolving drug abuse-related problems is in the best interests of public health and is key to eradicating stigma and discrimination. More awareness raising and trainings to communities, service providers, especial those in health institutions and the police service are key to addressing the problems of stigma, discrimination and ill-treatment of drug users as outcasts. Laws and policies that safeguard national borders from the smuggling of drugs need to be reinforced both in Zimbabwe and within the SADC region. Governments political will to design and institute, in collaboration with civil society, a harm reduction strategy in partnership with other stakeholders could be an example of effective partnership in health promotion. Most importantly, there is need for both leaders and citizens to accept the fact that an addiction is a medical condition requiring treatment, not incarceration.

Recommendations

Failing to address the rise in drug use will certainly have an adverse impact on not only the gains that we have made as a country as far as the HIV response is concerned but most importantly the rights of the concerned individuals in terms of harm reduction and rehabilitation. The current laws as they exist (for example arbitrary arrest) are punitive and not rehabilitative towards drug users and as a result drug use has worsened or gone underground. There is therefore a need to develop and implement a harm reduction strategy given the links between drug use and the HIV response. More specifically the following steps can be taken to avoid drug abuse across all age groups, especially among youths and key populations.

| Chapter Eight | Charles Mutasa |

1. More studies on drug users and abusers are required in Zimbabwe. There is need to carry out research aimed at providing evidence to specifically open up social spaces for dialogue on the Zimbabwe illicit drug situation at both local and national levels. Currently, for PWUD, Zimbabwe currently has no information on the estimate size of population HIV prevalence, ART coverage, condom use, coverage of HIV programmes and how many avoid accessing services due to stigma and discrimination for this group.
Organizations assisted drug users such as ZCLDN requires support inthe areas of capacity building particularly in the areas of documentation, advocacy, networking skills and diplomacy skills. This is important because the organisation needs to generate evidence to not only support its programming and advocacy work but also to ensure its relevance because responding to the problem of drug users has not been a priority of the government and other stakeholders. As noted earlier, the organisation needs to demonstrate the linkages between HIV and drug use through research and this can only happen once the organisation has the capacity to conduct and commission research.

2. How we address the problem of abuse of drugs that have legitimate medical use must necessarily differ from how we address illicit drug abuse.

3. As far as the PWUD there is no clear government position on how to address this growing problem in Zimbabwe. There is a need for drug reform by parliament, alignment of laws and legal systems to address drug use and criminalisation, identification of Drug users as KPs and the introduction of harm reduction as a strategy to treat drug users. ZCLDN as key informant stressed the need to reform the laws affecting drug abuse particularly Chapter 7 of the Criminal Codification Act because the law criminalises drug users. They went on to advise that the government needs to capacitate its workers – particularly the health and law enforcement officers (police and prison officers) because there are no rehabilitation services in prison and yet they often arrest people for substance or drug use. The government also needs to engage in partnerships and provide or

assist in accessing funding for organisations working to support drug users since this is a growing problem.

4. Zimbabweans in the diaspora should avoid being used as drug couriers.

5. There is need for effective drug education among young people, especially in schools and tertiary institutions so as to curb the problem of drug abuse in the bud.

6. A purposive capacity building programme targeting government officials and policy makers at both national and local government levels is vital to tackling stigma and discrimination of drug users in Zimbabwe. A focus on addressing the demand and doing little with the supply side may not take the nation forward in terms of addressing drug abuse.

7. For improved results, there is need to deliberately prioritise engaging political, religious, traditional and other community leaders to transform norms and attitudes that fuel stigma and discrimination against drug users.

8. Zimbabwe needs to be able to develop a programme to contribute towards the capacity building of government workers – particularly the health personnel and law enforcement officers with respect to service provision targeting drug users in the implementation districts.

9. Last but not least, improved integration of drug control programs with other health services in particular HIV treatment services, would increase effectiveness and provide a more in-depth understanding about how people who inject drugs are accessing and using treatment. These could easily be monitored and coordinated through the establishment of a Drug Commission that reports to parliament.

References

Anderson, T.L. 2017. Women's Evolving Role in Drug Trafficking in the United States: New Conceptualizations Needed. New Jersey: Rutgers University Press, 43

Anthony P. Jurich et al., "Family factors in the lives of drug users and abusers", Adolescence 20 (77): 143-159, 1985

Atega, T.H. (1998).Africa a Hub for Drugs. Cape Town, South Africa: the Mail Guardian

AYZ .2017. Drug Abuse: Lessons taken to School. See www.b-metro.co.zw (Accessed 2 March 2018).

Bhabha, Jaqueline. 2008. "Trafficking, Smuggling, and Human Rights". Migration Policy Institute: Washington.

Financial Gazette, Rampant drug abuse among Zim youths, January 29, 2015. http://www.financialgazette.co.zw/rampant-drug-abuse-among-zim-youths/ (Accessed 2 February 2018).

Goredema, C. 2011. Drugs and Violent Crime in Southern Africa; SADC Law Journal Volume1, 2011.

Gumbo.T. 2015. Teenage Sex Parties Stun Zimbabweans, Bulawayo24 News. See https://bulawayo24.com (Accessed 21 December 2017).

HSRC. 2016. Alcohol, tobacco and other drug use among black youth. Pretoria: Human Sciences Research Council.

IOM. 2009. Migrants' Needs and Vulnerabilities in the Limpopo Province, Republic of South Africa - Report on Phase 1 Nov-Dec 2008. February.

Jenner, M.S. (2011). International Drug Trafficking: A Global Problem with a domestic Solution; Indiana Journal of Global Legal Studies, Volume 18 Issue Number 2, Article 10, 2011.

Lawhub. 2017. Drug Trafficking in Zimbabwe. Criminal Law. See also (https://lawhubzim.org/drug-trafficking-in-zimbabwe/ Accessed 21 May 2018).

Mbatia, A. M. 2016. Drug Abuse Prevention: A Handbook for Educators. Dar es Salaam: Mehata Publishers.

Moyo, A. Zimra intercepts $10m drugs, in The Herald, July 20, 2018

Munodawafa, D. P.J. Marty and M. Gwede 1992. "Drug use and anticipated parental reaction among rural school pupils in Zimbabwe." Journal of School Health, 62: 471 – 74

National Drug Law Enforcement Agency. 2017. Battle Against Drug Scourge: Bamaiyi's Magic Wand. Lagos: NDLEA

Mutingwende, B. 2016. Substance and Drug Abuse Rampant among Zimbabwean Youths. Community Development Health. Zimbabwe Civil Liberties and Drug Network. See also http://spiked.co.zw/sub

stance-and-drug-abuse-rampant-among-zimbabwean-youths/ (Accessed 6 February 2018).

Narcotics Control Board (Ghana). 2017. Annual Report of the Narcotics Control Board, (Ghana).

National Aids Council, 2017. Annual Report. Ministry of Health and Child Care, Harare.

Paradza.K, Zim-students-nabbed-for-drug-trafficking-in-Cyprus, 4 June 2017, https://www.zimeye.net/zim-students-nabbed-for-drug-trafficking-in-cyprus/(Accessed 21 November 2017).

Rukuni, C. Zimbabwe to deploy drones to fight drug trafficking and smuggling, See http://www.insiderzim.com/zimbabwe-to-deploy-drones-to-fight-drug-trafficking-and-smuggling/ (Accessed 21 February 2018).

SAPA. 2008. "Porous Borders Need Sealing." [online] Available from: http://www.news24.com/News24/South_Africa/Politics/0,,2-7-12_2330771,00.html

Shleifer, A. and Vishny, R. 2015. "Drug Abuse", Quarterly Journal of Economics, Vol. 108, No. 3, pp. 599 – 617.

The Chronicle, "Mental Illnesses and Substance Abuse- Cause for Concern, "20 April 2017, p4.

The Herald, Harare's Drug Abuse Headache, 6 March 2017, p5.

The Africa Report.2011. 'Six Zimbabwean Women to Die for Drug Trafficking. The Africa Report.

Towo, A. The need for Scientific Research in the fight against Drug and Substance abuse in Zimbabwe, 11 January 2018, https://bulawayo24.com/index-id-opinion-sc-columnist-byo-125597.html (Accessed 13 February 2018).

Tsiko, S. Mental Illness and Substance Abuse Cause for Concern, The Chronicle 20 April 2017, http://www.chronicle.co.zw/mental-illness-and-substance-abuse-cause-for-concern/ (Accessed 11 December 2017).

UNDCP.2015. The Drug Nexus in Africa: Kenya, A Report for the United Nations Drug Control Programme , Nairobi: Kenya

United Nations, "Report of the United Nations Secretariat. Drug abuse: extent, patterns and trends", Prepared for the Commission on

Narcotic Drugs, thirty-seventh session, Vienna, 13-22 April 2014. (E/CN.7/2014/4, 21)

United Nations. 2000. "Protocol to Prevent, Suppress and Punish Trafficking in Persons, Especially Women and Children, Supplementing the United Nations Convention Against Transnational Organized Crime." UN: Palermo.

United Nations, "Report of the United Nations Secretariat. Drug abuse: extent, patterns and trends", Prepared for the Commission on Narcotic Drugs, thirty-seventh session, Vienna, 13-22 April 1994. (E/CN.7/1994/4, 21)

United Nations, 2013. The Drug Nexus in Africa. UNDOC, Vienna.

UNOC 2016, Zimbabwe Launches the Trafficking in Persons National Plan of Action and adopts the Blue Heart Campaign http://www.unodc.org/southernafrica/en/stories/southern-africa_-a-regional-response-to-smuggling-of-migrants.html (Accessed 2 February 2018).

UNDOC.1995.The Social Impact of Drug Abuse https://www.unodc.org/pdf/ technical_series_1995-03-01_1.pdf page 7 (Accessed 11 January 2018).

Wright, J.D. et al, "Health and social conditions of street children in Honduras", American Journal of Diseases of Children, March 1993, vol. 147, p. 282.

ZCLDN, National Capacity Strengthening Workshop on illicit drug use in Zimbabwe Support. Don't Punish Campaign 23 June 2016, Harare, Zimbabwe. See http://supportdontpunish.org/ wp-content/uploads/2016/08/Final-report-day-of-action-in-Zimbabwe.pdf (Accessed 6 February 2018).

Other Sources

FGD with PWUD group on Drug Abuse in Harare (aged between 21-42 years), 12 October 2017.

FGD with Sex Workers in Bulawayo, 21 December 2017.

Chapter Nine

The Impact of the Integrated Border Management (IBM) Programme on Promoting Contemporary Border Management at Zimbabwe's Border Posts

Solomon Muqayi and Rosemary Kasimba

Introduction

IBM can be divided into two categories: (1) domestic integration between government agencies within one country or customs union and (2) international integration between neighbouring countries. Both types require interagency cooperation, parallel processing, and coordination at ports, harbours, and land border points of entry (collectively referred to as ports of entry) for an optimal collective efficiency of these border institutions. For the second category, neighbouring or contracting national authorities must also cooperate with one another to align border-crossing facilities and procedures.

Customs administrations are usually best situated to develop integrated procedures for the processing of goods at points of entry. Border and immigration police focus primarily on the processing of people at those points of entry as well as the regulation of both people and goods attempting to cross borders illegally between those points of entry. Thus, the emphasis of IBM is placed within the customs process itself. The two types of IBM require a clear delineation of responsibilities for goods (customs) and passenger processing (immigration). While these responsibilities require different operations (for example, goods classification, carrier and goods inspection, revenue collection, and transaction verification for customs, versus visa verification, health, and anti-smuggling for immigration), the evolution of training and the use of technology have enhanced border integration and increasingly allow border officers to perform both functions. In most cases, a country will integrate its own processes before it initiates efforts to integrate with a neighbour or trade agreement partner.

The use of IBM as mechanism for facilitating trade is increasingly seen as an effective way of achieving policy coherence and coordination. This liberal interpretation of IBM is not really inconsonance with its historical context. The asserted genesis of the term extended from the Schengen use of common uniform principles for checks at EU borders and integrated approach to prevent criminals from taking advantage of borderless areas (Hobbing 2007). The external border rules however cover what is described in the succeeding sentences. For one, it relies on a unified organization of border agencies which makes coordination less cumbersome. The provision of services can be carried out in a synchronized manner, consolidated office hours are followed, and procedures harmonized. For another, it allows a more cohesive attention to the security aspects of trade through the use of common procedures, the possible single application of risk management system to determine inspection decisions, and standardized responses to security threats. Finally, it provides a single entry point for border clients and for possible coordination with neighbouring and trading partners in terms of border cooperation and collaboration.

IBM is therefore an organizational means for trade facilitation that ensures some coherence of policies and consistency of domestic and international transactions while at the same time maintaining strong security presence. The manner of this organizational structure may range from a complete overhaul of state apparatus (or applicable only in certain ports and borders) to agreements among different organizations to consolidate defined functions for trade facilitation. Mainly an organizational track of domestic institutions, IBM focuses on those that are involved in border responsibilities. For example, the reorganization of border agencies in the United States is partly an effort at the integration of border management – the creation of a Department of Homeland Security (DHS) and the consolidation of many agencies under a single roof. Moreover where there are traditional agencies with broader missions, inter-agency agreements allowed organizational set-ups at the port levels.

While there are directions for the use of IBM in trade facilitation, its actual routine application is primarily in police work, in ferreting out illegal migrants and entry of unauthorized people, in the detection of drug trafficking and smuggling of contraband goods, and other security-related functions. In fact, its origins can be traced to the progress of the unification of Europe which required the elimination of internal border checks and the development of common external border management (Hobbing 2005:6). On the other hand, before the combined emphases on immigration, police, and trade, the European Union (EU) had relied on customs to provide the coordinating tasks connected with border functions and management (before the emergence of the IBM term), that is, primarily trade facilitation. It is only with the advent of the security threats associated with 9/11 customs actively worked with police and border guards through cooperation. In addition the smooth flow of customs work into IBM, at least in the EU, has been a product of legal nuance (there is an established EU customs legislation in contrast to different legal orders to administer Schengen (Ibid.:7). There is therefore a basis for looking at IBM in the larger context of trade facilitation. Nevertheless the concerns in the EU surrounding IBM make it less appropriate in the tradition of trade facilitation as it is now understood (the efficient movement of goods across borders. This can be better appreciated when compared with the context found in other borders such as those in the North America and their underlying environment.

Conceptual Framework

The Concept of Globalization

There are three dominant views on the historical analysis of globalization: the sceptical view, the hyper-globalist view and the transformationalist thesis (Held et al, 1999). The sceptics argue that internationalisation and global connections are by no means novel phenomena. By placing cultural, economic, political, social and technological developments on an evolutionary time-line, the sceptics argue that globalization has existed for centuries and that the sum of recent developments only changes the scale and scope of globalization and not the intrinsic characteristics of the phenomenon itself (Martens et al., 2003). The hyper-globalists, on the other hand, do not deny the importance of previous bouts of globalization, but identify an historical juncture after which contemporary globalization emerged. The previous eras are sometimes described as pre-globalization or as periods of internationalisation. According to the hyper-globalists, contemporary globalization is fundamentally associated with the erosion of the power and authority of the nation-state (Held et al, 1999). The transformationalist thesis in some sense represents a compromise between the views of the previous two (Martens et al., 2003). The transformationalists argue that globalization is the major force underlying the rapid, widespread social, political and economic changes that are currently reshaping and reconstituting modern societies and the world order.

The nation-state still has an important, albeit transformed role. Each perspective on globalization emphasises different factors as the key elements behind the contemporary impact of this phenomenon. Moreover, each presupposes a different definition of globalization. In our opinion, rather than attempting to define globalization and determine its effects by emphasising particular aspects or factors, it would be far more useful to adopt a more multidimensional, pluralistic approach. This will prevent an over-simplification of the complexities involved in understanding globalization, while permitting a flexible definition of contemporary globalization. It is stating the obvious to declare that globalization has not suddenly appeared out of the blue. An understanding of the type of factors and events that shaped globalization will enable a better understanding of the overall context of the contemporary discussions about it. In this chapter, globalization is described and measured by identifying key economic, political, technological, socio-cultural and environmental landmarks that have accelerated the process of globalization over a relatively short time span in several societal domains. To preview, different aspects that underlie globalization are identified. These are: capitalism, technology, politics, the environment and social and cultural life. We restrict the number of key landmarks for the sake of clarity (Martens et al., 2003). This is not to say that other factors, events, processes and developments do not also influence globalization or would not also serve as appropriate key landmarks. The selection of the key landmarks serves, however, to constitute a sufficiently multi-dimensional and pluralistic approach.

Technological innovation as the engine of globalization

Technological innovations, particularly those in transport and communications technology, form a second primary foundation of globalization. According to Langhorne (2001), globalization originates in the second stage of the Industrial Revolution, with James Watt's invention of the steam engine in 1765 being pivotal. Langhorne (ibid) distinguishes three phases of technological innovation that marked the process of globalization. The first phase is characterized by the application of the steam engine to land and sea transport and the invention of the electric telegraph. Steamboats and steam locomotives significantly reduced transportation time and increased transport volumes. The steamship was introduced in 1807, while the first successful test of the steam locomotive was not until 1825. The construction of railroads connected cities, regions, nations and continents to each other, accelerating the pace of transportation. Moreover, this development increased the scope of industrial activities, thereby increasing the quantity of goods, the distances that goods could be shipped and people transported. It also made the distribution of information faster and less costly. The invention and improvement of the electric telegraph by Gauss, Weber and Morse between 1830 and 1850 separated the speed of communication from traditional forms of transportation for the first time. The latter represents an historical turning point in the development of globalization, since distances in space and time decreased significantly.

Nation states were able to react and to learn more quickly from the events that occurred in their national territories, including those in remote colonies. When the first Trans-Atlantic telegraphic cable was laid in 1865, it also sped up international communication. The invention of the telephone and automobile further enabled the nation state to increase control over its territories (Langhorne, 2001). The technological empowerment of the nation-state led to a homogenization between different regions within the nation's territory. Examples of this are the introduction of standardized clock times and national newspapers. Although this phase had its most profound impact on the nation-state, it also made international trade and financial contracting easier. Because of the technological homogenization processes, nation states commenced trading with larger and disparate geographical regions. In addition, international standards, such as Greenwich Mean Time, were introduced which improved timetabling and communication for international activities (Mackenzie and Wajcman, 1999).

The second phase began during World War II when German engineers working on the V-2 project invented rocket propulsion (Martens et al., 2003). After the War, the intense technological competition between the Soviet Union and the United States accelerated the development of rocket and satellite technology. The technological ability to launch rockets into space made it possible to launch orbiting satellites into outer space. Thus, a truly global and reliable communication system was established for the first time in human history. Although international telephone communication was previously possible, the connections were usually of poor quality. The widespread use of the telephone was therefore in large part restricted within national boundaries. Hence, the introduction of satellite communication exists as a bellwether in the improvement of international communication (Langhorne, 2001).

The last phase is the invention of the computer. Although the invention of the computer dates from as early as 1942, the capacities of the first computer barely exceeded the capability of today's hand-held calculator. However, the invention of the microchip in 1971 by Intel increased the speed, processing volume and efficiency of computers. Similar to the introduction of the electric telegraph, the invention of the microchip can be considered a major turning point in the development of globalization. The microchip forms the core of contemporary information and communication technologies. The development of ICT has led to a similar revolution, reducing distances in space and time, as the electric telegraph had done more than a century ago (Castells, 1997; Harvey, 1989). Further innovations and applications of the microchip have led to the emergence and widespread use of the internet and other computer communication systems. More importantly, the invention of computer technology and the microchip made it possible to construct global data networks that function as the hardware for the global financial capital market. According to Langhorne (2001), the invention of the computer and its widespread applications characterize the current phase of globalization.

Another important technological development has been the innovations in transport technology, such as container transport and passenger aircraft. Since the end of World War II, the international mobility of people and the international tradability of varieties and quantities of goods have increased dramatically. Although the rapid growth of international passenger flights and transport increased over a longer time span, a concentration of growth can be discerned in the 1970s (Loader, 2002:78). Overall, it needs to be noted that while Langhorne provides a convincing analysis of the role of technology in the process of globalization, his argument is technologically deterministic. By stressing the role of technology, Langhorne obfuscates the other factors and domains that also play a key role in the process.

Global Interdependence and Its Impacts

Borders are a popular scholarly topic since they define and make visible states, the basic political building blocks of regional and global systems. But has the stability of the Westphalian state system which emerged over the last four centuries been undermined by the increasing interdependence of states? One can argue that the growing interdependence of states, economies, cultures and populations, enabled by technology, has seriously eroded states' capacity to control personal mobility and the transmission of information and capital, and to assure the integrity of their borders (Martens et al., 2003:90). Legal economies have their illegal counterparts, the criminal activities conducted by transnational organized crimes which cannot be controlled by one state alone. Vast migrations flow across the globe as people seek jobs, attempt to escape massive local violence or flee from political persecution. States are in the world, and the world is in the states. In this view, the notion that borders still matter seems a quaint and outdated way of thinking. Borders are merely the crumbling remnants of sovereignty and will be washed away incrementally by the floods of legal and illegal mobility of people, goods and information.

Yet one can also argue that borders have become more important as interdependence offers new and enhanced opportunities for the mobility and global distribution of conventional and new threats. States still matter, and conflicts and tensions across the globe still depend for their management and resolution on state activities. Borders still define the state as the ultimate actor in dealing with threats to security, justice, rights and freedoms. No other agency can do what the state can do. A more complex perspective on borders is that they are simultaneously becoming more and less important; they matter less since the capacity of states to control the mobility of people, goods, services and capital has been seriously eroded and control has drifted away from states, or has to be shared with non-governmental agencies and groups (multinational corporations, transnational NGOs, IGOs and transnational policy groupings and communities) (Martens et al., 2003). At the same time borders retain their ultimate status as one of the defining characteristics of states, namely sovereignty over a limited piece of territory, and remain essential political building blocks of the global system.

In addition, since borders are guarded by at least two states, or a region and bordering states in the case of the SADC, views on what needs to be done (what is the problem) and how to do it (domestic and trans-border organizational arrangements, policies and priorities) are likely to differ by time and space, and will lead to patterns of cooperation which will fluctuate in salience and intensity as national priorities and political wills shift (Harvey, 1989). As IBM develops organizationally and operationally it will not and cannot be controlled by one sovereign state or a regional structure, unless the continent becomes the United States of Africa.

Border security systems are about more issues than security at the border. Their design and implementation are influenced not only by the reality of threats and security needs but also by how such threats are perceived, categorized, interpreted and integrated into a larger 'securitization' discourse (Loader, 2002); an extensive discussion of the rhetoric and normative content of the securitization discourse in the SADC can be found in Guild et al., (2008c). IBM in the SADC will evolve within a wider political discourse on the nature of threats, vulnerabilities and acceptable control policies. As internal border controls are eliminated, external borders and the increased threats from illegal activities and new, post-Cold War security threats have become crucial issues in policy discussions of what the enlargement of the SADC to include 'transitional' countries entails (Hills, 2005). The security discourse reflects widespread public anxieties, identifies strangers as threats to the well-being of SADC member states, supports and tolerates productive law enforcement techniques against security threats which would not be acceptable to members of the SADC and reinforces an emergent us-versus-them SADC identity. For example, under the Schengen regime which new members must accept, formerly open borders will now be closed to citizens left outside the Schengen space, creating a new 'iron curtain' (Anderson, 2000: 23) between the EU and its neighbours. In short, the structure, competencies and powers of IBM institutions as these are created will require domestic and transnational agreements among the 27 member states of the EU, and will be shaped by multiple political, objective and subjective factors.

Linked to the notion of securitization, but approaching the question from the perspective of good governance and democratization, are the fundamental reforms thought necessary to ensure democratic control of new border management institutions and policies (Loader and Walker, 2007: 195). The border control system and border police need to be subject to democratic oversight and governance, as do all security agencies which have the right to use force to control people. Specific accountability mechanisms have to be developed as new integrated border control strategies and institutions are being created. The exercise of accountability cannot continue to rest, mainly or solely, with current member states' mechanisms.

Methodology

This section discusses the research methodology that has been adopted to accumulate relevant data on the impact of the Integrated Border Management (IBM) in enhancing trade facilitation at Zimbabwe's borders. The major issues outlined in this methodology comprise of data collection methods and data analysis. Data gathering methods used in this chapter included are primarily interviews, documentary search and observations. A combination of secondary and primary data was used in order to compensate and mitigate the inherent shortcomings of employing one method (Creswell, 2003:43). Thus, primary and secondary data were engaged to offer a complementary significance to the data collected for the purposes of enhancing reliability and validity of data collected in the data collection process. The researcher conducted 20 in-depth interviews with officials from various organisations and governmental ministries such as the Zimbabwe Revenue Authority (ZIMRA), Ministry of Foreign Affairs and International Trade, Ministry of Industry and Commerce, Zim-Trade, Common Market for Eastern and Southern Africa (COMESA) Secretariat as well as Shipping and Forwarding Association of Zimbabwe (SIFAZ). The researcher also reviewed articles and primary reports from ZIMRA, Ministry of Foreign Affairs and International Trade, Ministry of Industry and Commerce, Zim-Trade, Common Market for Eastern and Southern Africa (COMESA) Secretariat as well as Shipping and Forwarding Association of Zimbabwe (SIFAZ). In social sciences, documentary search is a method that involves the use of wide range of documents such as books, journals, government publications, newspapers, magazines, letters, diaries, personal notes, biographies, essays, government pronouncements and proceedings, internet and policy documents (Punch 2008:190). The documents collected from various institutions were helpful in providing statistics as well as a historical background of the development of Zimbabwe's border management and trade policies. The study also applied observation method to collect primary data. The researcher conducted observations in key border posts in Zimbabwe including Beitbridge, Forbes border post, Nyamapanda and Chirundu OSBP. The researcher has been observing a variety of border coordination and linkage systems in order to identify whether there was any form of integrated management of border posts in Zimbabwe. The researcher applied qualitative content analysis to analyse data.

Discussion of Findings

The Integrated Border Management (IBM) is a strategy that is very common within the borders of European countries. IBM requires cooperation among all agencies and authorities taking part at the borders. The Integrated Border Management (IBM) is a programme being implemented by the Member States of various regional blocs. It is a product of regional integration. Zimbabwe is implementing the IBM under the guidelines of both COMESA and SADC. Basically, the IBM falls under the BEMS programme. The Ministry of Regional Integration and Economic Cooperation was mandated with the authority to implement the IBM programme. Lymo (2010:01) defines the IBM as a "National and international coordination among all the relevant authorities and agencies involved in protecting state interests at the borders to establish effective, efficient and coordinated border management in order to reach the objective of open, controlled and secure borders." The IBM is mainly focused on the management of personnel that is agencies at the ports of entry rather than the management of operations and processes. Thus, the IBM pays close attention to the cooperation and coordination of agencies at ports of entry. Just to clarify matters, however, the study observed that the difference between the IBM and BEMS is that the BEMS is a programme which is broader in the sense that it focuses on both management of border processes and operations as well as the management of border agencies. One can therefore note that the IBM helps to improve key management areas which are fundamental in border management and these include communication, information exchange and mutual assistance and cooperation between agencies.

The strategic goals of border management are to enhance the protection of national security, national economy, public health, plant health and animal health. Thus, state interests at the border involve the protection of national security, the enforcement of export and import restrictions, the enforcement of immigration requirements, the enforcement of SPS measures and technical standards (Lymo 2010:15). Effective border management helps to address the problems and challenges affecting nations at international level such as international terrorism, human trafficking, smuggling, and national insecurity, drug trafficking, possibility of importing dangerous plants, animals and unauthorised people. In order to reduce the highlighted problems, the IBM calls for border agencies to cooperate and coordinate when carrying out their operations. The responsibility to protect diversified interests is vested in the mandate of various state agencies involved in undertaking border operations and these include the police, defence, immigration, customs and revenue authorities and those involved in human, animal and plant regulations. Generally, each agent involved in the management of border operations carries out its own specific duties and responsibilities. However, the importance of cooperation and coordination between/among border agencies and between adjoining countries is indispensable and inevitable. For instance, border agencies at the ports of entry have to agree on several issues such as opening hours, the sequence of clearing people, and the vehicles. They must also establish arrangements for the sharing of border infrastructure, facilities and equipment. This actually helps to reduce border barriers such as border delays, congestion and the harbouring of irrelevant border agencies. The reduction of border barriers implies that there will be an improvement in trade liberalisation.

The IBM programme is centred on the cooperation and coordination between border agencies. Border agencies are comprised of people working at the ports of entry. The agencies are responsible for processing goods and people crossing the border as well as enforcing the regulations so as to avoid the smuggling of goods (International Organisation for Migration, 2013). Under the COMESA regional integration arrangements, the IBM programme focuses on three basic categories of cooperation and coordination between border agencies. These categories include the levels of coordination and cooperation such as intra-agency, inter-agency and international (cross-border) agency level.

Intra-Agency Cooperation

This involves the cooperation and coordination of border agencies within the same organisation, department or Ministry. Intra-agency cooperation and coordination involves both top-bottom and bottom-up information flow. Border agencies from the same department communicate, for instance, the communication channels that occur within the ZIMRA department from the head offices to the lowest offices (Shayanewako 2013). The top-down information flow is vital for updating subordinate offices pertaining to the management of borders. The bottom-up information flow is fundamental in that agencies at the lower offices such as border clearing agencies may have an opportunity to the report issues, experiences and challenges they face when carrying out their duties. This actually helps to improve policies and regulations relating to the management of borders. During the period covered by this study, it was noted that the ZIMRA agencies working at the Chirundu OSBP raised a complaint about the air conditioners that were not working and the ZIMRA headquarters office raised this to the inter-ministerial Committee border management negotiations. Thus, intra-agency cooperation is helpful in bringing up the challenges faced at the borders and such information could be effectively used for policy making.

During the period covered by the study, it was noted that intra-agency was not at its best at Zimbabwe's borders as there were several challenges. One of the challenges was that there was lack of effective cooperation between border offices and those head offices located in Harare. For instance, ZIMRA offices operating at the border were not quite linked to offices located in Harare (Shayanewako 2013). For example, traders involved in the car importation businesses were facing severe challenges especially when the documentation process is not done properly at the borders. In the event that the ZIMRA Harare offices realised that there were some errors in the car clearing process, the importer of the car is forced to go back to the border with the car in order to fix the problem yet the ZIMRA Harare offices are supposed to communicate with their counterpart border offices and fix the problem without necessarily having the car importer physically visiting the border. Thus, it is a matter of poor coordination and cooperation between these offices. In addition, if the Harare VID office department together with the CVR department fail to locate the engine number of a vehicle, the car importer is advised to go back to the border to correct that mistake. The viable alternative to this is to have the offices located in Harare given the mandate to handle such issues without sending the car importers to the borders. Sending importers back to the borders increases costs to the importers thereby reducing the level of profits they make. The study, therefore, advises the various governmental departments to improve the intra-agency cooperation and coordination between border offices and the inland offices located in cities and towns.

This Study also noted that there was lack of coordination and cooperation between border agencies from the same departments. For instance the security service officers working at the borders seemed to lack effective cooperation and coordination. The majority of traders raised the point that their consignments as well as they themselves were being searched by security agencies more than two times at the same border by different officials from the same department, for example, by the ZRP. The ZRP officers were scattered at the border posts thereby causing confusion, with their uncoordinated and rather frequent inspections at different points. There was no system that ensures that the traders were searched only once by the ZRP officers. The study also observed that there was no mutual cooperation between the ZRP offices that operate at the borders and those that operate inland. For instance, the vehicles with foreign number plates were searched at each and every roadblock and the drivers were also asked to produce all their documents. These roadblocks and inspections were actually annoying to foreigners visiting Zimbabwe. This situation inevitably scared off travellers, investors and traders. The study, therefore, suggests that the border police officers should coordinate with inland police officers so as to avoid the physical, mental and psychological harassment of foreigners in Zimbabwe. In addition to that, ZRP inspections should be conducted at specific points in order to avoid searching a person several times in one day.

Inter-Agency Cooperation

Inter-agency coordination is defined as the interaction and cooperation between and among border agencies from different departments, organisations or ministries. Inter-agency coordination occurs at different levels of hierarchy, both vertical and horizontal (Shayanewako 2013). Horizontal coordination entails the cooperation between agencies at levels such as branch offices, regional offices and head office for example, the ZIMRA head offices linking with the VID head offices or the ZIMRA clearing agent working at the border linking with the VID officer who also work at the border. Vertical coordination entails the interaction of agencies from different levels, for instance, the ZIMRA headquarters officers may directly communicate with the CID officers working at the border. Thus, vertical coordination makes it possible for low- ranked officers to communicate with higher-ranked officers from different departments. Inter-agency coordination is generally fundamental in improving the effectiveness of border management since it brings together agencies from various departments to work together. Shayanewako (2013:6) states that "such coordination is necessary to bring about harmony, unity of purpose and remove or discard role duplication between and among border agencies." Thus, coordination reduces barriers hindering communication between agencies while at the same time improving liberalisation and thereby enhancing efficiency at the borders.

The successful implementation of inter-agency cooperation requires the establishment of networking activities in order to bring agencies closer to each other. Thus, the government should enact laws that tend to promote issues such as the exchange of information between and among border agents, mutual use of databases, joint training, joint investigation measures, and joint preventative actions (Martens and Rotmans, 2005:56). This would eventually help to address border delays. Security agencies such as the army, the ZRP and CIO should cooperate effectively. Inspections and the searching of cross-border traders should be clearly defined. The way it was done during the period covered by the study was resulting in the embarrassment of traders. The government should also advise the security agencies to handle illegal cross-border traders with utmost respect. Conversely, some of the traders were subjected to torture, harassment and severe punishments with some being forced to pay bribes. The establishment of effective inter-agency cooperation therefore helps to reduce incidents of abuse of traders and travellers at the borders. This would therefore help to improve accountability and transparency in the operation of security agencies thereby leading to effective border management.

The study noted that ZIMRA had embarked on activities that enhance inter-agency cooperation. ZIMRA has been involved in the drafting of a Memorandum of Understanding (MOU) between ZIMRA and the agencies representing the business community. The major stakeholders that made up the business community were categorised into the following groups: trade promotion and facilitation; Small and Medium Enterprises (SMEs); Industry and commerce; Financial services; Information and Communication Technology (ICT) and telecommunications (Grosskurth and Rotmans, 2005). Generally, the majority of the traders evade the payments of duties due to the lack of an understanding of the importance of the national revenue collection system. The establishment of effective cooperation between ZIMRA and the business community therefore helps to improve trust, accountability, transparency and openness between these two stakeholders. This also helps the traders and other parties within the business community to have a better understanding of processes carried out by ZIMRA such as revenue collection and enforcement of import duties.

The main challenge to the effectiveness of inter-agency cooperation in Zimbabwe is the lack of an institutional framework. This has adversely impacted on communication and coordination between agencies from different departments and ministries. The government should also carry out the following activities in order to improve the effectiveness of inter-agency cooperation: (1) Design manuals and flyers; (2) Conduct training programmes; (3) Mount public campaigns and awareness programs; (4) Improve information flow between and among border agencies; (5) Exchange of reports that are in both hard copy and electronic format; (6) Conduct focal meetings and briefings.

International Cooperation

International cooperation refers to the cooperation and coordination between or among border agencies of different countries. The interaction of agencies occurs at international level. For example, at the Chirundu OSBP, the Zimbabwean and Zambian border agencies conduct joint inspections, joint investigations and joint patrols and share border infrastructure. It also involves the coordination of border agencies of one country with the agencies of regional organisations or international organisations that are involved in the management of borders. The basic example is that of the Trade and Information Desk Officer (TIDO) agent appointed by COMESA to facilitate the STR programme at the borders (Dreher et al., 2008). This study noted that the TIDOs operating at the Chirundu OSBP were interacting a lot with ZIMRA agencies through the granting of tariff exemptions to small scale cross-border traders.

This study noted that international agency cooperation can be split into three basic categories namely: (1) Cooperation of border agencies from both sides of the border. This kind of cooperation helps to improve day to day activities and operations at the borders. It also helps to reduce possible disputes that may arise regarding the movement of goods and people. For instance, at the Chirundu OSBP, both Zimbabwean and Zambian border security agencies work together to combat criminal activities such as smuggling, illegal migration, drug trafficking and human trafficking. (2) Bilateral cooperation between neighbouring states involves cooperation and coordination that occurs between states that share borders. This cooperation is made possible through bilateral agreements and MOUs, for instance. The bilateral agreement that was signed between Zimbabwe and Zambia in order to facilitate the management and running of the Chirundu OSBP has helped to facilitate the handling of several issues such as exchange of information, infrastructure development and sharing of border equipment such as scanners. (3) International organisations and multinational cooperation: this coordination involves the cooperation that takes place between border agencies and the agencies representing international organisations such as COMESA, SADC, ILO and UN, among others (Anderson, 2000: 23; Dreher et al., 2008). International organisations are vital in facilitating border management in that they provide a wide range of activities such as the funding of border activities. For example, international organisations such as COMESA and the UN help Zimbabwe and Zambia with advice and information on how to improve the management of the Chirundu OSBP.

During the period covered by this study it was noted that the Zimbabwean government was taking part in improving international agency cooperation. Thus, there were discussions and negotiations that were being carried out at regional level, in both COMESA and SADC to facilitate the exchange of data between the revenue authorities of the Member States (Loader and Walker, 2007: 195–233). During that period, the Zimbabwean government was negotiating to establish an MOU with the governments of Mozambique and Swaziland, respectively. Zimbabwe was also negotiating an MOU with the government of South Africa in order to facilitate interexchange of customs and enforcement data between the two Revenue Authorities. Cooperation and coordination of revenue authorities from different countries help in providing solutions to border delays through the improvement of the movement and flow of goods and services passing the borders. This would eventually help to improve trade liberalisation and improve trade facilitation.

Relationship Created Between ZIMRA and other Revenue Authorities

This study noted that regional organisations are playing a pivotal role in buttressing liberalisation as a way of improving border management. The COMESA REC has taken some initiatives in joining together the revenue authorities from different Member States. The COMESA has initiated the development of revenue authority committees in order to address the challenges related to the customs management. These committees are referred to as Joint operation Committees (JOC). Thus, ZIMRA is directly linked with other revenue collection authorities from Zambia, Malawi, DRC and Swaziland. ZIMRA officials at the borders have already put in place some committees which integrate revenue officials from both sides of the borders. These committees operate jointly in facilitating border management. They hold meetings frequently with the aim of sharing the experiences and challenges they face. The study noted that the JOC at the Chirundu OSBP was doing well in handling border challenges such as women trafficking, child trafficking, drug trafficking and tax evasion among other border challenges. However, the JOC was heavily challenged by resources constraints. It was observed that there was no constant donor to fund the JOC operations. The committee operated with limited resources and this was limiting its capacity in discharging its mandate.

The study observed that cooperation of border agencies at international level has to be managed with maximum sensitivity and intelligence since it involves two or more countries. There are risks of losing official secrets to neighbouring countries. Thus, the IBM programme is inextricably linked to international politics. Poor management of borders and border agencies may cause insecurity of nations. The governments should, therefore, educate border agencies on how to interact at international level so that they do not share sensitive information with agencies from other nations, wittingly or unwittingly.

Challenges affecting the Effectiveness of IBM

The effectiveness of the IBM was challenged by the existence of too many border agencies representing different governmental departments. Shayanewako (2013:8) identified the following agencies operating at the Zimbabwean borders: (1) Ministry of Finance (Zimbabwe Revenue Authority); (2) Department of Immigration Control; (3) Ministry of Agriculture, Mechanisation and Irrigation Development – Department of Plant Protection Inspection; (4) Ministry of Health and Child Care-Department of Port Health Inspection; (5) Medicine Control Authority of Zimbabwe (MCAZ); (6) Ministry of Agriculture, Mechanisation and

Irrigation Development- Department of Veterinary Inspection; (7) Zimbabwe Republic Police (ZRP); (8) Ministry of Transport: Vehicle Inspection Department; (9) President's Department; (10) Environmental Management Agency (EMA); (11) Zimbabwe National Army (ZNA). The study noted that all the departments specified above were deployed to Zimbabwean borders and airports. This was amounting to border delays as traders were to go through several processes and inspection at various points. There were many agencies with the mandate to enforce security at the border posts and these agencies were from different governmental departments such as the Zimbabwe National Army, the Department of Immigration Control, Central Intelligence Office from the President Office and the Zimbabwe Republic Police (CID Department).

During the period covered by this study, it was noted that the national legislation was not specific on the security agencies that were expected to carry out border checks and surveillance activities (Shayanowako 2013). This has resulted in the overlapping of authorities among/ between agencies. In addition, it was also noted that the legislation was not explicitly describing the limit, scope and authority of security border agencies. Ultra-vires this resulted in a situation that can be described as excessive abuse of authority by the security agencies. Such abuse, for instance, manifests itself as harassment of traders and travellers, executing unnecessary inspections and taking bribes, which is illegal. Furthermore, the security agencies were conducting their inspections haphazardly without cooperation and coordination. The government should, therefore, introduce a central point for inspections to avoid harassing traders and travellers. This can help reduce the adverse impacts of border delays.

The study noted that the major challenges constraining the effectiveness of the IBM programme at Zimbabwe's ports of entry were that: (1) there was no legal mechanism and framework formulated by the Zimbabwe government in order to facilitate the effective running of border management. Thus, there were no national policies, regulations or legislation establishing mechanisms for agency cooperation; (2) there was a lack of awareness programmes intended to educate the public (mainly traders and travellers) about the significance of the IBM programme; (3) lack of motivational benefits awarded to those agencies that adhere to the requirements of IBM (4) There was no Memorandum of Understanding regulating the operations of Zimbabwe's border agencies. It was indeed difficult to ensure effective cooperation and coordination between/among border agencies; (5) there was no formal legislation /agreement that specify the type of information to be shared amongst agencies. Due to the significance of national security issues, border agencies have a perpetual fear that if they share information with other agencies from other department they may be harassed or expelled by their superiors. Thus, border agencies were afraid of being accused of leaking official information.

Furthermore, it is difficult to choose which kind of information to share and which type of information to hold back. This led to situations whereby the border agencies were advised to seek consent from their superiors before releasing or sharing information with other departments. This study observed that the process of applying for permission to share information was long due to the bureaucratic nature of Zimbabwe's governmental structures and that there was a need of feedback which also took long to get. However, the processes of seeking consent in order to share information were not helpful in solving issues that require urgent attention at the borders; (6) Each agency was operating according to its own policies and procedures. Thus, there was no uniformity in the way in which agencies were operating. This was as a result of the absence of a Border Administration and Management Act; (7) there was no effective external communication frameworks and mechanisms that facilitate international cooperation of agencies; (8) there was unnecessary competition among the border agencies at both national and international level. For instance, Revenue Authorities from adjoining countries were embarking on stiff competition at the Beitbridge border post with South Africa Revenue Authority officers feeling that they were superior to ZIMRA officers due to their different salaries. This raised friction and tensions between these officials thereby reducing their interactions, coordination and cooperation; (9) the infrastructure and equipments found at Zimbabwe's ports of entry were not modern and therefore not compliant with the requirements of IBM; (10) the Zimbabwean government is not taking considerable efforts to teach border agencies on how to speak and understand different languages found within the COMESA region. Zimbabwe's border agencies are well-vested in Shona, English and Ndebele without having the ability to speak other languages found in neighbouring countries. Teaching border agencies several languages would be a cornerstone towards the achievement of effective regionalism. This will help to improve the levels of trade among COMESA Member States; (11) generally, there were weak and poor anti-corruption measures governing the operations of border agencies. There was a need to improve upon anti-corruption measures. The observed corrupt activities occurring at Zimbabwe's borders included: crossing ports of entry illegally; fraudulent obtaining of passports and visas; human trafficking; smuggling of goods, drugs, and weapons; abuse of discretion and favouritism; and (12) finally, there was no hierarchy revealing the chain of command among Zimbabwe's border agencies. This was creating confusion at the borders because all agencies felt that they are equal and it was difficult to exert control over these agencies. Henceforth, one can also note that the absence of a chain of command among the border agencies makes it difficult to monitor the activities occurring at the borders. The government should, therefore, appoint a special department that should be responsible for the overall border administration. This will help to improve the coordination and cooperation of border agencies thereby leading to the successfulness of the IBM programme.

The study noted that there was a need for strategies can be implemented in order to improve the effectiveness of the IBM programme and these are: (1) the government should carry out some monitoring and evaluation programmes at the borders as this can help to identify border agencies that are irrelevant and those agencies that deserve to be removed from the borders; (2) establishment of a department responsible for managing border activities such as carrying out the overall border administration as well as leading and coordinating all agencies operating at the borders; (3) the government should enact Acts and regulations that promote cooperation and coordination among border agencies; (4) Training border agencies to carry out several duties and responsibilities, can help to reduce overstaffing and duplication of efforts; (5) there is a need to develop by-laws, agreements and internal regulations that state each agency's responsibilities for more effective border management. This helps to clearly define the authority, task and responsibilities of each and every agent; (6) the government should issue mechanisms that define the rate of coordination and cooperation. There should be a clear outline of boundaries specifying the intensity of cooperation. In addition, the government should give an outline of the division of rights; and (7) the government should design frameworks and mechanisms in order to curb instances of resistance by agencies.

Conclusion

The increasing intensity of regional integration has resulted in the elimination and reduction of tariff rates and this has eroded the impact of tariff barriers thereby contributing to the emergence of harmful trade barriers referred to as NTBs. The most common types of NTBs that were observed at Zimbabwe's borders include: border delays, use of out-dated technology, lack of modern signage, corruption, physical and mental harassment, unnecessary inspections and searches, out-dated technology, bureaucratic pathology, existence of unnecessary border agencies and harassment (physical, psychological and mental) of traders. Generally, border protectionism has several negative effects such as retaliation by neighbouring countries; long queues at the borders; congestion at the borders and the scaring away of potential foreign investors. Local consumers are restricted to local products only given the lack of competition in the domestic markets.

It has been noted in this chapter that border management is one of the most significant aspects of a nation since it determines national security issues. Weak border management programmes usually lead to the nation's vulnerability to international threats like international terrorism, women trafficking, child trafficking, drug trafficking, and the economy will be under victimisation by international competitor companies. Thus, effective border management requires monitoring of goods and people entering and exiting a country. Border management is also used as an effective way of managing the national economy. Governments therefore impose some trade barriers at the border to protect the economy from international threats. The major programmes implemented at the Zimbabwean borders to address trade barriers at the same time enhancing trade facilitation include BEMS, OSBP, IBM and ASYCUDA. COMESA as a regional organisation has promoted the successful implementation of the highlighted programmes through: supporting research, funding, enhancing capacity building programmes and liaising with cooperating partners, among others. This Study noted that these programmes are effective in addressing border trade protectionism.

The major challenges affecting Zimbabwe's border management programmes are poor infrastructure, the dependency syndrome, bureaucracy, globalisation, lack of research, lack of Memoranda of Understanding entered into by the government to enhance border management, the prevalence of bogus border agencies since no authority has been appointed to direct operations at the borders, the absence of a border Act and the individualism among border agencies.

Recommendations

The basic strategies that should be implemented to improve border management in Zimbabwe are:

- Investing in research
- Application of automation technology to all border agencies
- Introduction of a help desk at Zimbabwe's borders
- Improving internet connectivity at the ports of entry
- Appointing an authority or department to oversee and monitor border operations.

The study, therefore, suggests that the implementation of these strategies could help improve the flow of goods across the borders thereby increasing the rate of trade liberalisation.

Reference

Bowman, G. W. 2006. 'Thinking outside the border: homeland security and the forward deployment of the US border', *Houston Law Review*, vol. 44, no. 2, pp. 189-251.

Creswell, J. W. 2003. Research design: Qualitative, quantitative, and mixed methods approaches. (2nd ed.). Thousand Oaks, CA: Sage.

Doyle, T. 2011. 'The future of border management', in G. McLinden, E. Fanta, D. Widdowson and T. Doyle (eds), Border management modernization, IBRD/World Bank, Washington, DC.

Hobbing, P. 2005. "Integrated Border Management at the EU Level", CEPS Working Document No. 227 (April). Brussels, Belgium: Centre for European Policy Studies.

Hobbing, P. 2007. "Management of External EU Borders: Enlargement and the European Border Guard Issue," in Caparini, Marina and Otwin Marenin (2007), pp. 151-173.

Lamy, P. 2003. 'Trade Facilitation in the new world trade environment' In: CosgroveSacks, C. and Apostolov, M. (eds.) Trade Facilitation: The Challenges for Growth and Development: United Nations, Geneva and New York. pp. 144-146.

Mitsilegas, V., Monar, J. and Rees, W. 2003. The European Union and International Security, Guardian of the People?, Palgrave Macmillan, London.

O'Dowd, L. 2002. 'The changing significance of European borders', in J. Anderson, L. O'Dowd and T. Wilson (eds), New borders for a changing Europe: cross-border cooperation and governance, Frank Cass, London.

Radelet, S. and Sachs, J. D. 1998. 'Shipping Costs, Manufactured Exports and Economic Growth. Cambridge Massachusetts: Harvard International Institute for Development, Harvard University.

Rippel, B. 2011. 'Why Trade Facilitation is Important for Africa', Africa Trade Policy Notes No. 27, Published by the World bank, Washington D.C. November 2011.

Shayanowako, P. 2013. 'Study into the Cooperation of Border Agencies in Zimbabwe'. Stellenbosch: Tralac.

Chapter 10

Human Smuggling from Zimbabwe to South Africa through Beitbridge Border Post

Lawrence Mhandara and Oripha Chimwara

Introduction

As the forces of globalisation intensify, transnational population mobility has also heightened, making migration increasingly prevalent in discussions of policy (Fisher, 2016; Karyotis and Sweparis, 2013). Today's world is deeply threatened by the effects of smuggling as a result of increased migration; a process associated with the movement of people from the less developed to the relatively developed countries. Neske (2006: 121) observes that human smuggling is part of the migration process closely linked with people's desire to seek opportunities to improve their living conditions, personal and political security. Kyle and Siracusa (2005) argue that smuggling exists because of the existence of borders which can only be crossed under stipulated legal restrictions imposed by states that far exceeds the demand for migration. Since the emergence of the state system, not all people travelled legally across borders but the number of smuggled migrants is increasing (Liempt and Sersli, 2013: 1031), prompting responses to counter smuggling. International law frameworks are categorical in criminalising smuggling. This is complemented by enhanced border management systems by individual states. Despite the efforts, human smuggling is still rampant.

The phenomenon of human smuggling in Southern Africa remains largely under researched (UNDOC, 2011: 25). Although the notion of smuggling is topical in both media, political and policy discourses in Zimbabwe. The focus of attention has been smuggling of commercial goods and services commodities from neighbouring countries without sufficient inquiry into the extent of the problem in relation to humans.

Great questions still prevail as to the elements of human smuggling in the context of perennial irregular migration to neighbouring countries, especially South Africa. Out of the estimated four million Zimbabweans abroad, three quarters are believed to be in South Africa, and 83%are categorised as illegal (Makina, 2012). The Global Commission on International Migration [GCIM] (2015) observes that illegal migrants in South Africa include those who enter and stay through smuggling. This makes smuggling a unique illegal activity that warrants separate investigation from other forms of irregular migration. The overall objective of this chapter is to enhance understanding of the elements of human smuggling from Zimbabwe into South Africa through Beitbridge border post.

Literature Review and Conceptual Framework

Literature on human smuggling is scanty compared to other illegal activities associated with migration such as human trafficking. At a sub-regional level, Southern Africa Development Community SADC has also supported and strengthened measures against irregular movement of people across borders. Smuggling or trafficking in persons is criminalised despite the absence of an explicit provision in the SADC Charter dealing with human smuggling. The SADC however adopted a 10 year Strategic Plan of Action on Combating Trafficking in persons, especially women and children (2009-2019). Through the action plan, the sub-regional grouping sent a clear message that its member states considered preventing and combating human smuggling as a priority that require special attention and solutions across the sub-region (SADC Secretariat, 2017). However, a good starting point in understanding human smuggling is the law itself. International law frameworks are categorical in criminalising smuggling of humans. Article 3 (1) of the Smuggling of Migrants Protocol (2000: 42) (a supplement to the United Nations Convention against Transitional Organised Crime) defines smuggling as "The procurement, in order to obtain, directly or indirectly, a financial or other material benefit of the illegal entry of a person into a state of which the person is not a national or permanent resident". Article 6 imposes an obligation on states to criminalise smuggling and the associated economic benefits from illegal immigrants. In terms of Article 5, the purpose of the Protocol is to criminalise smugglers and not smuggled migrants. The definition shows that the phenomenon of smuggling occurs when migrants are unlawfully assisted to cross international borders without the knowledge or consent of the receiving state. Smuggling of persons becomes a form of irregular immigration.

Irregular migration is described by the International Organisation for Migration (IOM) as involving irregular entry, overstaying and unauthorised work. Smuggling contributes to irregular migration through providing transport, illegal crossing and procurement of illegal travel documents (Heckmann, 2007). Why does smuggling occur and why is it prevalent even if it is illegal? The most dominant answer to the question is that smuggling is part of the illegal migration profit generation that is common across regions. Prominent scholarly voices in this view are Herman (2006), Salt (2000) and Stein (1997) among others who argue that smugglers are illegal entrepreneurs who commodify migrants. Smugglers become traders, while the smuggled migrants constitute their clientele who pay them for facilitating their illegal entry or stay in the destination country. Batsyukova (2012: 48) amplifies this point:

> The relations between smuggled and smugglers are commercial in nature, where the former is involved in the process to be moved to their 'country of dreams' while the latter gains profit from this illegal activity.

Smuggling is considered a form of crime perpetrated by profit-driven individuals or networks that include recruiters, transporters, informers and money launders (Schloenhard, 2002). In line with this view, smuggling can be considered a security threat not least because smuggling networks can coexist with criminal elements. For instance, there has been increased involvement of organised crime organisations into smuggling of migrants along the US-Mexico border, with fears that proceeds of smuggling activities can be channelled toward terrorism financing (ibid).

The rival perspective rests on familial ties as fuelling smuggling. This view suggests that migrants from countries of origin to the destination are connected through kinship, friendship and ethnicity. The ties reduce the costs and risks of migration (Herman, 2006). The perspective argues that family and friends play an active role in encouraging migration but also through facilitating illegal movements and assisting migrants to be integrated in the destination countries. In this way, smugglers will simply guide their clients towards their destinations. The migrant is viewed as an actor in the process and not merely an object. Therefore, the relationship between the smuggled and the smuggler is complex in that the smuggled migrant is not always recruited but voluntarily avails himself/ herself to the smuggler. Smuggling becomes possible because of conscious choices made by the migrant to enhance their lives in the destination countries. Van Liempt and Doomernik (2006) conclude that presenting migrants as passive actors who simply follow smugglers. Webb and Burrow (2009) argue that the reality that smuggled migrants rarely use the word 'smuggler' but prefer 'helper' instead demonstrates the complexity of the relationship. Indeed, sociological research is more concerned with the relationship between the migrants and smugglers, whose mutual interests make the process more complex than the traditional image of the merciless criminal (smuggler) and the passive victim-migrant (Van Liempt and Doomernik, 2006).

Since smuggling is a phenomenon that belongs to illegal activities that fall under the rubric of irregular migration, it has to be distinguished from human trafficking because the two are frequently used interchangeably in literature (Salt, 2000; David and Monzini, 1999). It has to be acknowledged that there are serious debates as to the relationship between smuggling and trafficking of persons. On one hand, there is a group of scholars who see overlaps between the two. The overlap is that smuggled migrants can be targets of considerable impunity by traffickers (Arowitz, 2001; Webb and Burrows, 2009). On the other, there are those who call for separation between the two based on characteristics. The second view is more persuasive than the first. Human trafficking is characterised as the transportation, movement, harbouring and receipt of persons through force, deceit, fraud, abuse of power to achieve the consent of a person having control over another person having control over another person for the purpose of exploitation (Article 3 (a) of the Trafficking in Persons Protocol). UNODC (2006) sets three characteristics of differentiating trafficking from smuggling. First, in trafficking, the source of profit is exploitation while smugglers extract their profits through facilitating illegal stay or entry. The smuggler and the migrant relationship normally ends upon the illegal stay or entry in a destination country. In contrast, the relationship between the migrant and trafficker subsists beyond illegal entry or stay in a country. Second, trafficking may involve the legal transportation or movement of persons and may occur within and across borders. On its part, smuggling is always illegal and can only occur across territorial borders. Third, smuggling frequently occurs with the consent of the migrant whereas trafficking thrives on force, fraud, coercion or deceit of the migrant. Batsyukova (2012: 42) argues that smugglers and the smuggled migrants are both offenders who break the immigration laws of the destination country. In contrast, trafficking operations violate the rights of the trafficked. In this case, the trafficker becomes the offender. However, the relationship between the two is that trafficking can start as smuggling (a person gives consent to be smuggled and later be the target of an exploitative relationship by the smuggler).

This chapter conceptualises smuggling challenging border management because of the consequences both to the smuggled migrants and the states whose citizens are smugglers or smuggled (smuggling may lead to human trafficking, insecurity to the receiving state due to its contribution toward irregular migration).

Methodology

The chapter provides insight into human smuggling as a stand-alone challenge in the context of emigration of Zimbabweans to South Africa. The focus is on the explanatory factors of illegal migration through smuggling, profile of the smuggled migrants, the actors and the *modus oparandi* in smuggling operations. The overall objective was to generate relevant information that would assist Zimbabwe first and foremost to respond to the menace. Given the clandestine nature of smuggling, using conventional research methods with the primary actors in the smuggling operations was herculean. Nonetheless, interviews and informal conversations were conducted with key informants to provide insight into the elements of human smuggling through Beitbridge border post. The key informants interviewed were three immigration officers at the Head Office of the Zimbabwe Immigration Department, while informal conversations were held with two cross-border traders, two bus operators and two drivers at Harare's Road Port Cross-Border transport station.

Specific questions were posed to the nine respondents to generate primary data that addressed the objectives of the research as follows:

- What are the specific factors that push Zimbabweans to migrate to South Africa, legally and illegally?
- What is the role of human smuggling in promoting migration to South Africa?
- Who are the people targeted by smugglers or willing to be smuggled, including age, education, social background and so on?
- Who is actually involved in human smuggling through Beitbridge border post?
- How do smugglers carry out their operations through Beitbridge border post?
- What are the consequences of smuggling to both South Africa and Zimbabwe and the smuggled migrants themselves?
- What do you think the government of Zimbabwe should do to counter human smuggling through Beitbridge border post?

Primary data was complemented by secondary literature to construct the thematic narrative in the findings and discussion section.

Research ethics were upheld for they serve a duality of purpose in academic inquiry: safeguarding the integrity of the research; and safeguarding the interests and rights of the targeted respondents. As a starting point, information about the research objectives, how the data would be used, who would have access to the data and how anonymity of participants would be protected was provided to all the nine respondents who partook in the research. Interview and informal conversations transcripts were anonymised by removing any information that may identify a respondent by name and replaced with pseudonyms. Anonymity was important to safeguard respondents' identity given the criminal nature of smuggling. Most of the respondents were initially suspicious of the researcher's motives. Suspicion was minimised by assuring all respondents that all the data collected was confidential and was solely for the research and shall be kept between them and the researcher. Through informed consent, respondents were also informed of their right to refuse to take part in the research and verbally consented to participate. In addition, the ethic of voluntary participation was observed by ensuring that no respondent was forced to divulge any information related to smuggling against his/her will.

Findings and Discussion

The Reality of Migration of Zimbabweans to South Africa

This theme emerged out of responses based on the question: *What are the specific factors that push Zimbabweans to migrate to South Africa, legally and illegally?* Respondents highlighted that the border between Zimbabwe and South Africa was imposed by colonialism because the people in the two countries had long been migrating back and forth. Migration to South Africa was seen as part of the historical fact that people have been for long freely moving across communities. Tapiwa, a respondent amplified this point: *The movement of people* (migration) *is not a new thing. It is a historical occurrence where people had the choice to move from one place to the other for various reasons. It is the same thinking that may be forcing Zimbabweans to go to South Africa. Unfortunately, the movement is not that easy these days.* The sentiment by the respondent shows that migration of Zimbabweans to South Africa is viewed as natural as people have for long moved from one place to another for various reasons. This suggests that migration is a phenomenon that has been imbedded in the history of human society. However, where migration occurs, it can be viewed as the result of the intercourse between individual choice and environmental constraints (Mhandara and Chimwara, 2017).

Further responses on the question also show that people were migrating to South Africa for a variety of reasons. Respondents were of the view that the situation in Zimbabwe was forcing people out of the country. Simon said:

I'm not sure what happened around the year 2000… *(inaudible)*. But what I know is that this is the period when I began to notice some negative developments. The political players were mobilising against each other including through violence across the country. The industries, farms, shops, everything was going down. It was unbelievable for some of us who had never experienced that. Life was becoming unbearable. That's when I started to notice people running away from the country going to Botswana, Zambia, UK, South Africa and everywhere trying to survive.

From Simon's response, it can be surmised that people have been flocking to other countries mainly for political and economic reasons.

The challenges that faced the country since the turn of the millennium are well documented and provide an adequate explanation as to why Zimbabweans would choose to emigrate. Migration in Zimbabwe is motivated by negative political and economic developments forcing people to go abroad or sponsor family members to migrate to economically stable countries to improve their living conditions, education and economic opportunities (McGregor, 2007: 806 in Bloch, 2008: 3). Bloch (2008: 4) concludes that the influx of migrants from Zimbabwe to other countries is mainly a consequence of a combination of economic or employment related reasons than others. Political instability was also cited by respondents as an explanatory factor to the migration trends. In general, the socio-economic and political forces in Zimbabwe constrained individual choices and contributed to insidious forms of everyday suffering (Morreira, 2010: 436).

The response to the unbearable political and economic environment in Zimbabwe forced people to migrate in large numbers to South Africa which they considered a 'dream' destination within the region. John had this to say:

There was no hope and the problems were worsening by each day. Children were not going to school, families needed to be fed. People began to explore opportunities elsewhere and South Africa became the preferred destination because of too many menial jobs –farms, restaurants etc. The buses were loaded as if no one was willing to stay in Zimbabwe anymore. Very few had the required papers *(legal travel documents)* and most were just going without anything.

The combination of worsening political and economic situation pushed Zimbabweans abroad but mainly in South Africa because of the vast opportunities for casual employment. The purpose of migration was purely survival, primarily economic and employment reasons. Indeed, Zimbabweans responded to the challenges by migrating in large numbers to destinations within the SADC region and beyond (UNDP, 2010 in Makina, 2012: 368). Of the estimated quarter of the country's total population designated as migrants, two-thirdsare hosted by South Africa (Makina, 2012: 368). "Migration to South Africa is a well-established household poverty reduction strategy" (Black et al, 2006: 116), because of the economic challenges that Zimbabwe has been experiencing resulting in large-scale migration (Morreira, 2010: 433). The economic and political challenges in Zimbabwe, combined with the proximity of a relatively stable South Africa, cajole Zimbabweans to emigrate in large numbers, legally and illegally. Besides, the trend has a historical explanation in that migration is seen as intrinsic to the developmental process of Southern Africa because of the pronounced history of labour migration into South Africa's mining industry (Tati, 2008). South Africa has always held a unique place within the vast tapestry of the African diaspora. More so, the new structures of global production consider South Africa as an emerging economy together with Brazil, India, China, Russia, collectively called BRICS. South Africa has been a hub for economic migrants than war refugees attracted by its relatively thriving economy (fordhampoliticalreview.org). The increased movement of people within the SADC region is also inevitable with agreements such as the SADC Protocol on the Facilitation of the Movement of Persons in place, and economic ties and interdependency growing.

With more people opting to migrate to South Africa, the legal migration route became overwhelmed and the requirements were tightened. This prompted illegal entry alternatives to be considered by the desperate Zimbabweans. This was noted in the responses to the question: *What is the role of human smuggling in promoting migration to South Africa?* Sam elaborated:

When many people were crossing the border, South Africa was alarmed by the number of Zimbabweans in their country. They tightened requirements for work permits and entry. It became difficult. That's when people began to use other means to just cross the border. Whatever happens thereafter was not a concern as long as they were out of Zimbabwe. The cross-border transport operators 'helped' (smuggled) a lot of people to enter without the papers *(illegally)*. Some would just go to Beitbridge were they were 'helped' by people in Beitbridge to cross the border through the Limpopo river.

The response suggests that as the legal means of entry into South Africa were tightened, Zimbabweans resorted to illegal ways of entry. Instead of reducing the number of migrants into South Africa, tight border control contributed to the soaring illegal migrants amidst crisis in Zimbabwe.The situation of Zimbabwean illegal migration worsened that it is described as a 'revolving door syndrome' where illegal migrants are deported and then return (Waller,2006 in Bloch, 2008: 9). The response also alludes to the availability of smuggling services asa key contributor in compounding illegal migration.

Profile of Smuggled Migrants

The question posed to respondents that yielded this theme was: *Who are the people targeted by smugglers or willing to be smuggled, including age, education, social background etc?* Zimbabwe has a population of more than 14 million people, of which 60% are aged between 18 and 35 years (SADC Secretariat, 2017). Out of this, respondents indicated that the majority of smuggled migrants were young people, with a small proportion of underage persons. This was indicated in John's response who noted that: *"Most of the people whom I see in the smuggling operations are mostly young and some very young that I wonder where they will be going. Most of the smuggled migrants are male and a few ladies. There are also a few middle and old-aged people who are smuggled. Some will be working in Zimbabwe but most are not working. They will be just trying to survive."* The situation is unsurprising considering that youth unemployment is acknowledged as a global challenge (International Labour Organisation, 2013).

It is acute in Zimbabwe because of a mal-performing economy that has one of the highest unemployment rate in the world at 95% (World Factbook, 2017). This means that young people in Zimbabwe are easily attracted to employment opportunities abroad as their own country offers little or no opportunity for self-actualisation. The difficult economic conditions in the country was cited as encouraging young people graduating from high schools and tertiary institutions to migrate to South Africa because of its perceived economic opportunities. The migrants face severe underemployment and unemployment. In terms of their social and education background, there is a reported diversity among the smuggled migrants. However most smuggled migrants hail from disadvantaged backgrounds, with the right job skills and education but they face uncertain future due to lack of formal employment opportunities. Both sexes, although majority are male, are willing to be smuggled as they seek to overcome the lack of prospects for self-actualisation. There is also a strong perception for both the working class and the non-working skilled young Zimbabweans that South Africa is seen as the best option to improve their livelihoods.

Actors and Modus Operandi

Data show that human smuggling through Beitbridge border post involves a number of actors. There people who coordinate the smuggling operations. The coordinators normally work with migrants who have weak or no connections in South Africa and assume overall responsibility for the illegal entry. The coordinators have many contacts from the migrant's point of departure to both sides of the border post. The coordinator is assisted by people who market the smuggling services and sets contacts between the smugglers and the smuggled before the operation begins. The people who market the services work with a number of smugglers to maximise their profits. The more migrants they recruit, the more their profits. The process of marketing smuggling is usually accompanied by deliberate misinformation to migrants, many of whom have never visited South Africa, regarding the requirements for legal entry, conditions and opportunities in the destination. Araia (2009: 16) argues that migrants often enter South Africa illegally after being misled by smugglers who do not advise them of the opportunities to enter the country legally. Makina (2012) reinforces this opinion by arguing that the misinformation and deliberate omissions of smugglers create an imaginary border which in the minds of migrants is far more antagonistic and forbidding. This encourages migrants to see smuggling as the only means to enter South Africa. The smuggling services are marketed at popular cross border stations in Harare, Bulawayo, Gweru, Masvingo, Mutare and Beitbridge. The recruiters work closely with drivers of cross border vehicles mainly buses and cargo trucks.

The cross-border bus drivers also assume dual responsibility of transporting and coordinating the smuggling operations. The drivers are acquainted with the border control procedures and they have also co-opted border management authorities at either side of Beitbridge border post through bribes to allow the migrants free passage using the legal entry points. "Corruption officials are paid regular stipends and bribed on an ad hoc basis to allow the passage of illegal migrants and facilitate illegal stay. Some officials are also actively involved in providing their own smuggling services and conspiring to extort money from illegal migrants" (Araia, 2009: 47). Indeed, there is a smuggling service wholly provided by the police, which provide passage directly through the legal entry route (ibid). The amount paid to police officers is normally 200 rand per migrant. This effectively means border management officials are also actors in the smuggling operations. The officials include the police, military and immigration officers who are paid a bribe to facilitate the illegal process. Most of the smuggling that happens through Beitbridge is small scale that does not involve all the identified actors in one operation. Rather, smugglers are tempted to arrange all aspects of the operation themselves to maximise profits.

It also emerged that most of thesmuggling operations are not pre-planned and smugglers are approached at either side of the Border by clients without the legal documents or seeking illegal stay in South Africa. Thus most of the smuggling happens in an ad hoc manner. Migrants are also assisted by family members, fellow immigrants and friends at no cost to cross illegally. In most of the cases, the smugglers bribe port authorities to smuggle the migrants, either as their clients or friends or relatives. The smuggling fees are not fixed but migrants with no contacts in South Africa can be charged between 1200 and 1500 rand (Informal conversation with Joseph). The border towns of Beitbridge in Zimbabwe and Musina in South Africa also serve as bases for onward travel by smuggled migrants. The typology of human smuggling is not a sophisticated industry; it is a loose network of a few service providers well connected to border management officials, following adaptive and flexible tactics that are difficult to detect. By and large, the key actors in smuggling operations are transport operators and drivers of cross-border passenger transport, fellow migrants, friends, relatives and border management officials, who assume the role of coordinators, recruiters and marketers.

The Need to Counter Smuggling

Smuggling of migrants challenges the capacity of both governments to manage migration and the ports of entry. Smuggling also undermines South Africa's acceptance of Zimbabwean migrants as legitimate. Zimbabweans feel that South Africans take advantage of their desperation and the fact that most were illegally staying in the country to exploit or abuse them (Informal Conversation with Nathan).Thus although Zimbabwean migrants constitute a small proportion of the South African population, the scarcity of resources feeds discourses that posit all foreigners as illegal (Morreira, 2010: 437). The prejudice is also official. For instance, South African Police often harass, assault and extort money from Zimbabweans and fail to verify their legal status before ill-treating them (Human Rights Watch, 2006). The South African government has adopted a tone that has framed the migration problem through a security angle. Over the years, Zimbabwean migrants have attracted a growing negative perception with a striking semblance of anti-immigration attitude. As the number of immigrants increase and the economy weakens, tensions between foreign nationals, primarily Zimbabweans, and South Africans have escalated. One dominant official response by South Africa is that Zimbabwean illegal migrants are a threat to social order and stability. The argument is that there is an explicit link between Zimbabweans and a surge in crime. Government actors have come up with the criminal-migrant argument which demonises Zimbabweans as generally criminal, amounting to representation of all migrants as a unitary group, glossing over the distinctions between illegal and legal migrants (Mhandara and Chimwara, 2017). This affects every Zimbabwean in South Africa, who easily becomes soft targets of public anger and xenophobia. The increase in criminality in the South Africa is viewed as a correlate of the upsurge of mass illegal migrant flows into the country from Zimbabwe. The increased alienation and prejudice against Zimbabweans underscores the urgency to rethink appropriate strategies that counter human smuggling which is contributing to the illegal migrant catalogue in South Africa.

The securitisation moves by South Africa authorities is an expression of the rise of a continuum of negative effects associated with illegal migrants. The responses of South Africa through enhanced border control strategies and profiling of Zimbabweans as dangerous migrants has of late contributed to the disruption of free legal movement of migrants between the two countries, interfering with bilateral relations, and even regional integration. In this line of reasoning, smuggling of Zimbabweans into South Africa through Beitbridge border post represents an existential threat to bilateral relations. Smuggling may also contribute to yet another problem of human trafficking. Crawford (2016) heralds that Zimbabwean women smuggled to South Africa in search of better life do not always realise their dreams. Some are held by smugglers in the township of Diepsloot in Johannesburg, subjecting them to crude exploitation through forced prostitution.

Policy Implications

Anti-smuggling policies are legitimate. Emphasis must be that the *modus operandi* of smuggling operations is highly flexible and evolve to evade improved border management strategies. Strengthening border management capacity should also be accompanied by an insight into the root causes of smuggling, which forces smugglers to adapt their operations. Indeed, "... policy proposals have oversimplified the causes of human mobility and overlooked the potentially grave consequences of increased investment in border controls" (Araia, 2009: 6). Increased tightening of immigration controls is unlikely to succeed in controlling clandestine migration. It may worsen corruption while engendering illegal migration. There is need to investigate and punish corrupt officials at the border. Bilateral efforts between Zimbabwe and South Africa are in order since government officials on either side of the border are implicated in facilitating human smuggling. It is also important for the Zimbabwe government to engage its South African counterpart to ease the legal immigration requirements in the spirit of implementing the SADC Protocol on the Facilitation of the Movement of Persons to discourage recourse to illegal entry through smuggling. Such efforts must also be accompanied by public education campaigns in Zimbabwe and the border post on the legal opportunities available for migration to South Africa. This is necessary to debunk misinformation perpetrated by smugglers to potential migrants about South Africa's immigration processes.

Conclusion

Today's world is deeply threatened by the effects of smuggling as a result of increased migration. Smuggling exists because of the existence of territorial boundaries that can only be crossed under stipulated legal restrictions imposed by states that far exceeds the demand for migration. Despite tightening of migration policies and border management systems, human smuggling is still rampant. The Global Commission on International Migration [GCIM] (2015) observes that the illegal migrants in South Africa include those who enter and stay through smuggling. Yet great questions still prevail as to the elements of human smuggling in Zimbabwe in the context of perennial irregular migration to neighbouring countries, especially South Africa. This chapter provides insights into the dimensions of smuggling of Zimbabweans to South Africa through Beitbridge border post.

On its part, smuggling is a criminal and illegal activity under international law. This is explicit in Article 3(1) of the UN Smuggling of Migrants Protocol (2000). Unfortunately, smuggling is still prevalent. This is explicable in two main ways. Firstly, smugglers are viewed as illegal entrepreneurs who are motivated by financial gains by charging fees on migrants who are willing to gain entry illegally. In this view, migrants are considered as victims and smugglers are seen as offenders. Second, smuggling is rife because of familial, kinship, and ethnic ties that facilitate illegal entry at low or no cost. In this case, migrants are viewed as active actors in the smuggling process. While smuggling is just as illegal as trafficking, the two are distinct based on three characteristics:

- In trafficking, the source of profit is exploitation while smugglers extract their profits through facilitating illegal stay or entry;
- Trafficking may involve the legal transportation or movement of persons and may occur within and across borders. On its part, smuggling is always illegal and can only occur across territorial borders; and
- Smuggling frequently occurs with the consent of the migrant whereas trafficking thrives on force, fraud, coercion or deceit of the migrant.

In the case of Zimbabwe, political and economic considerations loom large in pushing Zimbabwe into illegal migration to South Africa through smuggling. Zimbabweans take this route because of the perceived relative stability of the economy and the prohibitive immigration policies of South Africa. Young people who have just graduated from high school and tertiary institutions are willing to be smuggled. The gender composition is mixed but dominated by males. The search for empowerment opportunities among youths is inevitable given the high rate of unemployment and underemployment in the country. The actors involved in smuggling are varied but cross-border passenger transport, cross-border traders, families and friends, assisted by corrupt border management officials at the border post, are key actors in the smuggling operations. The smuggling processes are frequently ad hoc and not sophisticated but highly flexible.

Besides undermining the capacity of both South Africa and Zimbabwe to manage migrants, smuggling also threatens bilateral relations between the two neighbouring states because of the securitisation of Zimbabwean migrants by South African people and government officials. In addition, smuggling exposes migrants to the risk of being soft targets for traffickers. Unfortunately, tightening border management systems alone cannot solve the menace on its own not least because smuggling operations are highly flexible and evolve to evade systems. The need to counter human smuggling in a holistic manner is urgent. This also includes the call for the Zimbabwean government to engage its South African counterparts with a view to ease the requirements for legal migration.

References

Araia, T. 2009. Report on Human Smuggling Across the South Africa/Zimbabwe Border. MRMP Occassional Paper. University of Witwatersrand: Johanessburg.

Arowitz, A. 2001. Smuggling and Trafficking in Human Beings: The Phenomenon, the Markets that Drive it and the Organisations that Promote it. *European Journal on Criminal Policy and Research* 9 (1): 167-195.

Batsyukov, S. 2012. Human Trafficking and Human Smuggling: Similar Nature, Different Concepts. *Studies of Changing Societies: Comparative and Interdisciplinary Focus* 1(1): 39-49.

Bloch, A. 2008. Gaps in Protection: Undocumented Zimbabwean Migrants in South Africa. Migration Studies Working Paper Series. London.

Crawford, A. 2016.Zimbabwean women Smuggled and Sold as Wives in South Africa.*Sky News*, 23 August.

David, F and Monzini, P. 1999. Rapid Assessment: *Human Smuggling and Trafficking from the Phillipines*. United Nations: New York.

Fisher, K. M. 2016. Disrupting the 'Conditional Selfhood' of Threat Construction. In: Hom, A., Mcintosh, C., Mckay, A and Stockdale, L. eds. *Time, Temporality and Global Politics*. Bristol: E-international relations publishing.

Global Commission on International Migration (GCIM). 2015. Migration in an Interconnected World. *New Directions for ActionReport*. GCIM: Geneva.

Heckmann, F. 2007. Towards a Better Understanding of Human Smuggling.IMISCOE Policy Brief No. 5.

Herman, E. 2006. Migration as a Family Business: The Role of Personal Networks in the Mobility Phase of Migration. *International Journal of Migration* 44 (4): 116-147.

Human Rights Watch. 2006. South Africa: Zimbabwean Migrants Vulnerable to Abuse. US Fed News: Washington D.C.

International Labour Organisation (ILO). 2013. Global Employment Trends for Youths on the Impact of the Global Economic Crisis on Youths. Geneva: ILO.

Karyotis, G and Sweparis, D. 2013. Qui Bono? The winners and losers of securitizing migration.*Griffith Law Review.* 683-706.

Makina, D. 2012. Determinants of Return Migration Intentions: Evidence from Zimbabwean Migrants in South Africa. *Development Southern Africa* 29 (3): 365-378.

Mhandara, L and Chimwara, O. 2017.The Securitisation of Migration in South Africa: Exacerbating Insecurity Intuitively (Unpublished).

Morreira, S. 2010. Seeking Solidarity: Zimbabwean Undocumented Migrants in Cape Town, 2007.*Journal of Southern African Studies* 36 (2): 433-448.

Neske, M. 2006. Human Smuggling to and through Germany.*International Migration* 44 (4): 121-163.

Salt, J. 2000. Trafficking and Human Smuggling: A European Perspective . *International Migration* 38 (3), Special Issue, No.1.

Salt, J and Stein, J. 1997. Migration as a Business: The Case of Traffickin g. *International Migration* 35 (4): 32-79.

Schoenhardt, A. 2002.Organised Crime as Migrant Smuggling: Australia and the Asia Pacific.*Research and Public Policy Series* 44. Canberra: Australia Institute of Criminology.

United Nations Office on Drugs and Crime. 2011. Smuggling of Migrants: A Global Review and Annotated Bibliography of Recent Publications. United Nations: New York.

United Nations Office on Drugs and Crime. 2006. A Short Introduction to Migrant Smuggling. *Issue Paper* United Nations: New York.

Van Liempt, I and Sersli, S. 2013. State Responses and the Migrant Experiences with Human Smuggling: A Reality Check. *Antipode* 45 (4): 1029-1046.

Van Liempt, I and Doomernik, J. 2006. Migrant's Agency in the Smuggling Process: The Perspectives of Smuggled Migrants in Netherlands. *International Migration* 44 (4): 143-187.

Webb, S and Burrows, J. 2009. Organised Immigration Crime: A Post-Conviction Study.*Research Report* No.15. London: Home Office.

* 9 7 8 1 9 0 6 7 0 4 9 0 2 *